ESCAPING *THE* HOLOCAUST

One Family's Flight from Vienna to Shanghai and Beyond

Compiled and Annotated by
Helen Weiner Betts

Translated by
Joseph Feitler

www.Helenbetts.com
Cover picture: The author and her grandmother

ISBN: 1450526918
ISBN-13: 9781450526913

ACKNOWLEDGEMENTS

My deepest gratitude and love goes to my mother, who kept these letters in a little cardboard box for seventy years. She must have known how important they would be some day.

My cousins: Joseph Feitler, who did a heroic job of translating the letters, and Eleanor Feitler, who remembered details about Vienna and our grandmother and her recipes; Uli Knoepflmacher, who translated his father's letters and provided some of the details of our history, as did Paul Schratter; George Pick provided the story of his uncle, Egon Stern.

Jessica Moll asked many questions as she edited, and suggested that I help the reader with more footnotes.

My daughter, Suzanne Curlis, my granddaughter, Siera Curlis, and my friends, Dorothy Witt, Nancy Boyarsky, and Chris Ford read and made suggestions and cheered me on.

James R. Ross and Renata Polt read parts of the book and encouraged me to continue.

So many people have been helpful and encouraging that I cannot name them all, but I am truly appreciative.

CONTENTS

Erna
Vienna – 1902

PREFACE

When my mother, Käthe Weiner, died in 2007, I found among her papers a small box labeled "Old Letters." Stuffed inside were crumpled, fragile air letters, dated from 1938 to 1946. As I carefully unfolded and straightened them I realized I had opened a treasure.

The letters, written in German, were typed, margin to margin on the finest tissue paper. Some were from my father's cousins and friends in Vienna, recounting their desperate struggles to find safe haven away from the advancing Germans. But most of the letters were from my grandparents when they first arrived in Shanghai and from my grandmother after the end of WWII.

My first challenge was to put the letters in chronological order, and then try to learn to whom the names belonged and their connection to the history of my grandmother and the many people who were connected to my parents, my brother, and to me.

. . . .

In October 1938, Käthe and Rudy Weiner with their two small children, my brother and me, were the first in their large circle of Jewish family and friends to escape Austria after the German Anschluss, the annexation of Austria by the Nazis. Our family settled in Chicago, where our apartment became a base for others who followed us to America.

My grandparents, Erna and Hans Mayer, were finally able to leave Vienna for Shanghai in November 1940. Their first letters, describing life in Shanghai and their pleasant lodgings, were almost cheerful. They wrote that life was much as it had been in Vienna. Already in place was a European community dating back to 1862, in which they felt comfortable and where they had business connections from the Mayer textile operations in Vienna.

In the afternoons the gentlemen gathered in the coffeehouses to play cards and visit with friends. Erna baked Viennese pastries, which she sold to the coffeehouses to earn a little income. But reading between the lines of these letters, I gained a different impression of their life, of their helplessness, boredom, and worry about the fate of relatives. Erna left a great deal out of her letters. I think that she did not want to burden her children with complaints. She often referred to the inflation in Shanghai where the high cost of necessities worried her. Years later when Erna's grandson, George Glauber, introduced his new wife, Talu, to the family, she was told she could ask anything about Erna's life except about the war years.

In 1946, when she was able to leave Shanghai, Grandma came to California and moved into our home. She took on the cooking, baking, and darning of socks. During that busy time of growing up, my brother and I didn't ask many questions about Grandma's years in Shanghai or about our parents' departure from Vienna. My mother often said that she had tried so hard to forget those experiences that she had actually succeeded. Grandma lived until 1975, and though her English got much better, she never spoke about Shanghai.

While reading my grandmother's letters, I felt as if we were finally becoming acquainted. As I searched for missing pieces of her story, I studied our family trees and have included abbreviated versions to help identify some of us. My Aunt Gusti was the keeper of the family lore. Before her death at age 101 in October 2007, I made many telephone calls to New York to ask her questions. I have included Käthe's notes that she had made for a talk given to her granddaughter's high school history class and excerpts from Gusti's informal autobiography that she typed on her tiny portable typewriter, in response to the family's many questions about her childhood and family history.

In September 2009, I went to Shanghai with my brother's son, Jon Weiner. Our purpose was to see what we could find of our grandparents' experience in Shanghai. We were pleased to find Bubbling Well Road in the French Concession in Shanghai. My grandparents lived there for two and a half years before they were forced to move to the ghetto of Hongkew in 1943. Erna was able to move back to the Bubbling Well area in 1946 after the war ended. Bubbling Well Road had been a main thoroughfare in Shanghai. The name has been changed to Nanjing Road. There is still a Bubbling Well Lane with a plaque commemorating its important past. The lane is closed to visitors, but my nephew, who speaks Chinese, asked the guard if we could go in and we were allowed to do so. It is a pleasant wide court-yard with a few tiny gardens and the ubiquitous laundry hanging from the windows on long poles. We took a guided tour of Hongkew, the area that had been designated by the Japanese occupation author-ities to restrict the residence and business of the thousands of state-less refugees who had arrived in Shanghai since 1939. There we saw the miserable conditions of the hutongs (alleys) where my grandpar-ents had to live at first. Later they were able to move to a somewhat better arrangement in a converted factory on Point Road at the edge of Hongkew. We looked for their address, 1106 Point Road, but the building has been torn down and replaced, as have most of the old ghetto buildings. In a small park in Hongkew there is a plaque dedi-cated to the "thousands of Jews [who] came to Shanghai fleeing from Nazi persecution..." We learned that the cemeteries where many of the refugees were buried have been dug up. The grave stones were stolen and are being found all over Shanghai, as door stops, in walls and entry ways.

In the last remaining synagogue in Shanghai, which is now a mu-seum, we found the register of stateless refugees. I felt a chill when I saw my grandparents' names inscribed there.

Heinrich Mayer 1106 Point Road

Ernestine Mayer 1106 Point Road

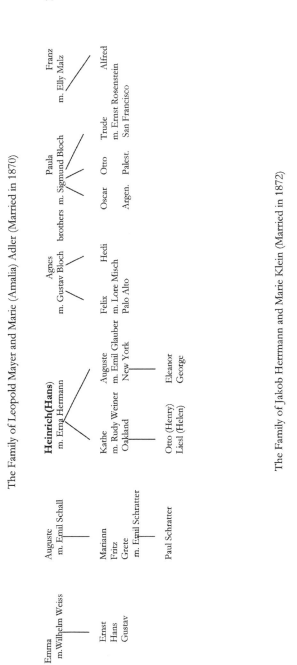

The Family of Leopold Mayer and Marie (Amalia) Adler (Married in 1870)

The Family of Jakob Herrmann and Marie Klein (Married in 1872)

INTRODUCTION

Ernestine (Erna) Herrmann was born in the city of Pilsen in 1884 in what was then the Austro-Hungarian Empire. The native language was German. Erna was the youngest of the five children of Jacob Herrmann, a prosperous businessman and one of the founders of the Pilsner Urquel Brewery. The family lived on the upper two floors of a large house on the city square, across from the cathedral.

When Erna was twenty-one she married Heinrich (Hans) Mayer of Vienna who was ten years older than she. He and his brother, Franz, managed the Leopold Mayer Bleiche, Farberei Und Appretur (bleaching, dying, and fabric finishing) concern that had been founded by their father. Heinrich had four sisters and two brothers.

The plant was situated in Kagran (emphasis on the last syllable) in an outlying district, the twenty-first, of Vienna. According to Erna's daughter, Gusti, "the plant was a huge building with a big garden, a very spacious courtyard filled with apricot and cherry trees where chickens could roam around and five horses were in a stable, with the necessary horse-drawn vans to deliver the finished goods." Its tall smokestack could be seen from miles away. Houses and apartments for the family and employees were also on the property.

Hans and Erna lived in an apartment on the grounds of the plant in the same building as Hans's mother Amalie, the doyenne of the family. She tended the flowers and chickens in the park-like surroundings, helped in the family business, and hosted the many family gatherings. When Franz was called up for military service in World War I, Erna took over the bookkeeping for the business. She insisted on doing the billing and payrolls without adding machines or typewriters although these were available at the time. She started work at 7 a.m., stopped for lunch with Hans at 1:30, and worked again until 7 p.m., while the nursemaids cared for the children.

Mayer Family Kagran 1918
Amalia Mayer, Trude Bloch, Gusti, Franz, Käthe, Hans,
Oscar Bloch, Mariann Schall, Grete Schall

Vienna ca. 1929
Fred Neubauer, Gusti Mayer, Käthe Mayer, Richard Neubauer

Erna enjoyed her office duties and continued with them full time after her two daughters were born. Auguste (Gusti, Gucki) was born in 1906 and Käthe in 1909.

Gusti and Käthe were educated at local schools. In addition they were given private lessons in French, music, and dancing. On holidays they went skiing and hiking in the Alps with groups of friends.

Gusti married Emil Glauber, an engineer from Tachau (emphasis on the first syllable), a German-speaking village in Bohemia. Emil came to work for Gusti's father, designing machinery and supervising production in the factory. He was appointed general manager in 1937.

Käthe married Rudy Weiner, who was managing the commercial laundry, the E.W.D. (Erste Wiener Dampfwäscherei) that had been founded by his grandfather. They too lived in Vienna in an apartment on the grounds of the plant.

"Tante Erna" welcomed the families of Gusti and Käthe into the Kagran circle of extended family.

In 1926, when Rudy was twenty-one, his father sent him to America to learn about commercial laundries similar to theirs. At that time he made contacts with some distant relatives in Chicago and with people in the laundry business. These contacts were a great help when the family emigrated from Austria.

In March 1938, Germany annexed Austria (the Anschluss). The Nazis occupied Vienna. Gusti witnessed the arrival of the German troops and observed the hearty welcome they were given by the Austrian people. Realizing the danger that Austrian Jews faced, she insisted that her family leave. She and the two children, Eleanor and George, aged eight and five years, left in September 1938 for Belgium. Emil followed shortly, and the family lived in Antwerp for a year before coming to the United States.

The Nazis took over many businesses, including the Mayer factory and the E.W.D. They imprisoned Rudy twice, in May and in June of 1938, as hostage for the plant, which they wanted to take over. Finding that they needed him to operate the laundry, they released him. Meanwhile, Käthe made daily trips to the Gestapo offices trying to complete the paperwork necessary for the family to be permitted to emigrate from Austria. The Nazis finally agreed to let the family leave if they would pay the departure tax and sign over the E.W.D. to the Germans. Käthe took the responsibility for signing over the business. The family went by train to Switzerland, then Paris and Amsterdam, where they sailed on the Vollendam for New York in October 1938 (one month before the historic Kristallnacht).[1]

Rudy was then thirty-three years old. Käthe was twenty-nine. Their children, Otto and Liesl, were five and two when they left Vienna bound for Chicago.

Most of the remaining family in Vienna and Kagran left as quickly as possible. Erna's nieces went to England. Her brother Max went to Canada. Her sister Clara remained in Vienna and Paula was still in Pilsen. Käthe's cousin Oscar Bloch went to Argentina, his brother, Otto, to Palestine. Several of her cousins came to America. Rudy's cousin Georg Knoepflmacher settled in Bolivia. Other family members went to Australia and Ecuador. Over the years they rebuilt their lives and prospered. Many of them were able to visit each other in their new homes.

In November 1940, delayed by a medical emergency requiring surgery, Erna and Hans were finally able to leave Vienna for Shanghai, the only place in the world that was still allowing Jewish refugees to enter.

In Shanghai, they continued the immigration application process to enter the United States. By November 1941, all their papers were in order. They had been given an appointment at the consulate for a final medical examination on 11 December. After the bombing of Pearl Harbor on 7 December, they learned that all visas had been invalidated and everyone would have to start all over again. From that date there was no more mail or travel between Japanese-occupied China and the United States. Four years passed before Erna could again begin to apply for entry to the United States.

---

1   Kristallnacht, November 9, 1938, the Night of Broken Glass, was the German Pogrom against the Jews during which thousands of Jewish businesses, synagogues, and homes were destroyed.

In 1943, all recently arrived Jews in Shanghai were forced by the ruling Japanese government to move, within ninety days, to the over-crowded, run-down, one-square-mile area of Hongkew. The Japanese, allies of Germany, had occupied the Nationalist cities of Shanghai and Nanjing since 1937. The forced move to Hongkew was a compromise with the Germans, who wanted the Japanese to deport all Jews to concentration camps in Europe so they could be included in the Germans' plan of ethnic cleansing.[2]

When the war ended in 1945, Erna was again able to write to her daughters and receive mail from them. Only then could she tell them about the death of their father, a few months before the end of the war.[3] During her final year in Shanghai, Erna wrote weekly, telling of her daily life during the war years and afterward, as she made her way alone without Hans.

Erna was finally able to sail for California to join Käthe and Rudy and her grandchildren, who were then ages thirteen and ten, in August 1946. Once settled, she enrolled in English and sewing classes and kept house for the family She also helped Rudy with the bookkeeping for his small laundry business, and occasionally did babysitting and housekeeping for neighborhood families. For a few months

---

2   The following story may be apocryphal. There were several versions of it: As World War II intensified, the Nazis stepped up pressure on Japan to hand over the Shanghai Jews. Warren Kozak describes the episode in which the Japanese military governor of the city sent for the Jewish community leaders. The delegation included Amshinover Rabbi Shimon Sholom Kalish. The Japanese governor was curious: "Why do the Germans hate you so much?"
"Without hesitation and knowing the fate of his community hung on his answer, Reb Kalish told the translator (in Yiddish): "*Zugim weil mir senen Orientalim* — Tell him the Germans hate us because we are Oriental." The governor, whose face had been stern throughout the confrontation, broke into a slight smile. In spite of the military alliance, he did not accede to the German demand and the Shanghai Jews were never handed over."
According to another rabbi who was present there, Reb Kalish's answer was "They hate us because we are short and dark-haired." *Orientalim* was not likely to have been said because the word is an Israeli academic term, which was not part of the Torah greats' language.
From Wikipedia. *Shanghai after 1937*

3   She wrote very little about the conditions in Hongkew. There was a severe shortage of food, medicine, and sanitary facilities. There were deaths from starvation and disease. Refugees had been forced to give up their businesses and employment. They were not allowed outside of the restricted area without permission, so were unable to earn a living. James R. Ross in Escape to Shanghai

each year, she traveled to New York to be with her daughter Gusti and her family.

In California and New York she often had visits from the Viennese family members and friends who had settled in various parts of the world. The hospitality of Kagran continued. During these visits guests were always served Tante Erna's Viennese specialties: Linzer Torte, Gugelhupf, and Vanille Kipferln with coffee. She translated her recipes from grams and kilograms to teaspoons and cups so that her grandchildren and their children could continue the tradition. Her great-granddaughters baked and served Linzer Torte for Käthe's memorial service in 2007.

PART ONE

1938 Vienna to Chicago

Käthe and Rudy were the first in their circle of friends and relatives to settle safely in the United States. They became the touch point for others who were lucky enough to escape Austria. By the end of 1938 they had found a large apartment on the south side of Chicago. It had three bedrooms, a "maid's room," which they rented to a fellow immigrant, a butler's pantry, a sunroom, and space for the grand piano, as well as for the heavy furniture and the household goods that they had shipped from Vienna. Rudy was employed in a linen supply business, and Käthe gave massages to private clients and baked cookies to sell in the neighborhood grocery store.

In spite of their own financial insecurity, they helped many of their relatives by providing them with affidavits of support,[4] which were required by the U.S. Immigration Department.

The following letters from Rudy's cousins and friends recount their efforts to leave Austria. They continued to gather in Kagran at the home of Käthe's parents, Erna and Hans Mayer.

---

4   Affidavits of support could be provided by legal residents of the United States. The sponsor was required to prove that he had financial means and could assume responsibility for the immigrant if necessary. Immigrants were still required to wait for their immigration quota numbers to come up.

STATE OF CALIFORNIA)
COUNTY OF SAN FRANCISCO) ss:

Now come RUDOLPH WEINER and KATHIE C. WEINER and they and each of them do aver and say:

(1) That they RUDOLPH and KATHIE C. WEINER are husband and wife residing in Oakland, California; that they have two children aged twelve and ~~three~~, and that besides themselves and the children there is no other person depending upon affiants for support other than KATHIE C. WEINER'S mother, ~~ERNESTINE MAYER~~ and R.W.'s mother to the extent of one third;

(2) Affiants further state that ERNESTINE MAYER, mother of affiant, KATHIE C. WEINER, is dependent upon affiants' support to the extent of one-half the sum necessary for her living expenses, the other half being contributed by a sister of affiant, KATHIE C. WEINER, namely Lusty Glauber 111-25 76 th Drive Forrest Hills N.Y.

(3) Affiants finally state that they have in their own names cash amounting to $1,000.00 (one thousand) such cash being free from all liens, claims, or encumbrances of creditors; that affiants own in their joint names a house worth $8500. (eighty-five hundred dollars), situated at 1359 Hill a # 5th .... of 5,000 # Mortgage ; and that the affiants own personal property to the extent of one Buick Automobile worth 750.00 free from all lien Furniture and Parisian Rugs and Jewels ... estimated at worth of about 4,000.00 free from all lien claim or encumbrances of creditors and War Bonds of the following Face values and dates of ....

Subscribed and sworn to before me
this _____ day of _____ 1945.

_____
NOTARY PUBLIC

Affidavit

1938 Vienna
From Hans and Edith Weiss[5]

My dear ones,

We are utterly embarrassed and therefore at a loss for words to thank you for your helpfulness and efficiency. We are delighted to note that your feelings for us have demonstrated the depth of our relationship; we have always had warm feelings for you. This has been particularly obvious for the last few months, and especially when we said good-bye. The emotional rift of the farewell touched me deeply. We are also convinced that you and we have done everything feasible to work our way out of such a tragic situation. But now it remains a big question if we could accomplish the same thing by ourselves. But you have achieved that goal—and so quickly at that—that you leave us breathless. And so now our sincere feeling of gratitude is getting mixed up with a certain pride in your ability to succeed. We are most eager to find out what you have accomplished, who actually provided your affidavit, etc. etc.

We are keeping up with your reports most eagerly. Thus there is a perfect interchange of information with people interested in your experiences. It gives us the greatest pleasure to "eat up" your letters; we also read them to our friends when we are lucky enough to receive a letter and have it in our hands for a few hours—it is an unwritten law that each letter is to be forwarded as quickly as possible. All of us are delighted with your good fortune. The facts seem to be so positive and favorable that all of us find renewed courage and hope for what lies in the future.

When we really think about our situation here, we can barely consider the possibility that you, after just such a short time in the United States, will be able to secure an affidavit for us In our current state of desperation we have been utterly honest with you when we pleaded with you to try to get us an affidavit. We were totally startled by Rudy's telegram; it was almost as unbelievable as Aunt Tillie's

---

5   Hans Weiss was a first cousin of Rudy. Settled in New York.

move back. This telegram has freed us from a deep depression and a very heavy load of worries. I don't think that we need to write to you what such an affidavit means for Egon[6] and us!!

We already know that you, Rudy, have a new job; we want to congratulate you on that achievement. We assume that you are very happy and that you could remain in your prior business; we like the idea that you have a good job. We also want to congratulate you, Käthe, on restarting your career in massage therapy; I (Edith) am so envious that I could light a fire! On the other hand, I have been downgraded to student at Rothschild Hospital.[7] I am taking a course there that cannot hurt me, but the main reason is to receive a certificate from that hospital.

We just had a very strenuous week when we moved from our apartment into a furnished room; we sold some of our furniture, some of it we gave to a transportation firm, and we took some of our possessions such as a couch, a drafting table, and some small stuff. There was terrible confusion during this move; we just didn't know where we stood. But you know all about that yourself, or perhaps you yourselves can still remember that experience. You probably heard from Egon directly about his plans. When we talk about Hella's[8] plans, they are still very uncertain; but, gradually, she will gain a better understanding of the United States.

It was very nice of you to worry about our affairs while you were traveling to Switzerland, Paris, and New York. It was also particularly good of you to get in touch with Aunt Mary.

So now we have been greatly encouraged that there now is some hope that we will see you very soon and throw our arms around you.

Yours very gratefully
Hans and Edith

---

6   Egon Weiss, brother of Hans. Settled in New York.
7   Rothschild Hospital was Vienna's Jewish Hospital.
8   Hella Hahn, a first cousin of Rudy. Settled in New York.

25 October 1938 Vienna
From Kurt and Edith Weiss[9]

Dearest friends,

Yesterday the last remaining people in our circle of friends (Imre, Else, Trude, Edith, and I) gathered at the home of your dear parents in Kagran. While there, we seemed to have forgotten everything in the outside world within a very short period of time. We felt that it was like old times, except for the fact that you were absent. In spirit we seemed to be in your presence; as you can imagine we were talking about you almost all the time. Your parents were so utterly considerate of us, a really touching gesture, and prepared a wonderful supper for us young ones. We left them with very heavy hearts. We had to promise them that we would visit them again before our departure; we have full intention to do so. Thanks be to God, your parents looked fairly good; they appear to be recovering slowly.

Perhaps you are already aware of the fact that we received a telegram in mid-month from our sponsor in Sydney; we were told that our permit had been authorized. Now we hope that before long we will be able to treasure this document in our own hands. You undoubtedly can appreciate what this news means to us, coming after several weeks of utter desperation and a series of upsetting events. Now at least we know where we are supposed to travel, a real big step ahead. To our regret, in the meantime Rolly and Edi[10] did receive negative news from "down under," a very depressing turn of events; they will be unable to stay in P any later than the end of this year. Using an Australian attorney, they have resubmitted their application in Canberra; we hope that we will be able to support their effort personally as soon as possible.

Our proposed departure date will depend entirely on when we can get our hands on the permit. Only then will we be able to book

---

9   Kurt and Edith Weiss were friends of Käthe and Rudy. They settled in Australia.

10   Edi Rauchberg and his brother Willi were close friends of Käthe and Rudy. Edi settled in Australia and changed his last name to Rogers. Willi settled in San Francisco and changed his last name to Rawley. There is no information about Rolly.

our passage. And this arrangement will not be easy, since there are only a few tickets available. In any case we know our destination; we have always been eager to travel to Australia. You might not be aware of the fact that meanwhile Edi has already received his Australian permit. We look forward to the great pleasure of meeting them down under in the future. In Edi's case there seems to be a problem in having the money to pay his landing fee and perhaps also the cost of his ticket. But we have been unable to receive a clear answer to our questions. Furthermore, Lotte and Leopold P. are desperately waiting for a positive response from Australia. They are eager to meet a nice number of friends down under.

We are delighted that you are doing so well, and that Rudy has already found a job. That fact is absolutely wonderful; you have truly earned this reward.

Thanks be to God, we can report only good news to you. Everl is becoming more lovable day by day, is exceptionally lively, but does not like to eat. She is already getting a few teeth; perhaps that is related to her eating problem. She is changing so rapidly that you probably could no longer recognize her. Perhaps we will have a future occasion to send you a new picture of little Eve. Currently we have been hearing good news from Greterl, but she seems to be very sad because her husband was transferred to Belgrade. So now they have to give up their beautiful apartment in Zagreb. But then everybody seems to have personal problems. Let's hope that she'll never have worse problems.

How are your children doing? Has Burschi[11] already gotten used to his new surroundings? How is sweet little Lieserl[12] doing?

You cannot imagine how much we enjoyed your postcard from Rotterdam, particularly because your predictions about dear Rudy proved untrue at the most critical time. You will probably meet many friends in Chicago, such as Dr. Pollaczek and his family. If you are interested we can provide you with their address. He is a particularly nice person.

---

11   Burschi (little boy) refers to Otto, later Henry, Hank Weiner, Käthe and Rudy's son
12   Lieserl, Liese, later Helen Elise Weiner Betts, Käthe and Rudy's daughter

But now I have to close because Edith would like to add her part. So now I want to conclude with the most sincere regards and kisses for you and your dear children

Yours
Kurt

My dear Käthe, and dear Rudy,

Kurt already mentioned above how much we enjoyed our visit with your dear parents; now I just want to repeat that same feeling. Though belated, dear Käthe, please accept my heartiest birthday congratulations in this manner. I was really thinking of you on the twelfth of this month. But we always seem to miss the important dates when we are so far apart. Kurt also sends you his belated wishes. We wanted to write to you about very positive things but since we have to scrimp on postage costs, we held off on our reply for a little while, and now the delay seems to have been very worthwhile. It is amazing how small the world is! As we can deduce from your letter, you have had various meetings with friends, some planned beforehand and others by sheer accident. We hope to have the same experience in the future; after all, it feels so wonderful to meet some old friends from the "old country." Do you feel very homesick? Have the kids gotten used to their new environment? How are you doing with your new language? We hope to hear more details from you when you can spare the time.

Evi is almost one year old; and I just don't know where the time has gone. To our regret we don't even have a single picture of your children, we would be very grateful if you could send us a picture of either one at your next opportunity. A long while ago we took lots of pictures; that really helped us to stay in touch with our friends, even if these pictures included some landscapes. For the time being we are still members of a steadily shrinking group of friends; we mutually read various letters about diverse topics to one another, just to keep mentally in touch with our far away friends and acquaintances.

Earlier today we found out that Gretel will arrive next week and plans to stay here for two weeks. You can imagine how we are really looking forward to her visit. She has been away for only three months, but that seems to be an eternity. Rolly makes sure to let us know how interested she is in little Eve; obviously she is very lonesome without her. Her only wish has been to travel to Australia with her niece. She is always deeply touched when we send some pictures. They have already been gone for four months, and we just can't get over the fact how fast time runs or the thought that we can in a few days enjoy seeing Gretel again. One cannot imagine the feeling of being far away and then awaiting the next arrival, especially if several years have elapsed in the meantime.

I want to wish you the very best for the immediate future; after all, that is usually the most difficult time. And after you have survived this particular phase, then everything will turn out well thereafter.

Heartiest greeting and kisses from your
Edith

12 November 1938   Vienna

From Georg Knoepflmacher[13]

Dear Rudy,

I telegraphed you yesterday: "Rudolf Weiner / 4625 S. Drexel Boule-vard / Chicago Ill. / Request affidavits. /[14] Birthdays: 8. February 1894 Vienna; 18 August 1895 Vienna; 26 June 1931 Munich. / Georg."

You know that I am not fond of grandiose and attention-seeking gestures. And precisely because you know that, I hesitated for quite a while to wire you my request for an affidavit, fearing that it might alarm you.

But on the 11th of November a letter confirmed that my personal chances for Portugal are none too high; and yesterday I discovered that the factory project had been cancelled. Therefore, at least on the second front, I am back to where I had started. Besides, there are rumors circulating here that the United States might be willing to lift quota deferments and allow an immediate entry to all existing applicants who can secure an affidavit.

Please believe me when I say that I do not ask for your help without an awareness of the enormity of my imposition. Nor do I ask you without full knowledge that more than your good will may have to be involved in securing such an affidavit. But I feel duty-bound to move all levers, and am bitterly aware that I may be placing heavy burdens on the shoulders of friends.

I have been told that the "San Francisco Committee for Service to Emigrants — 1600 Scott Street, San Francisco" may be able to achieve

13   Georg Knoepflmacher was a first cousin of Rudy. He and his wife Hilda and son Ulrich (Uli) settled in Oruro, Bolivia where he became a mining engineer and later became the Dean of the Engineering School at the University in Oruro. Uli came to the University of California at Berkeley in 1951. He lived for a short time with the Weiners. He became a Professor of English at Berkeley and later at Princeton. This letter and the following from Georg were translated by Uli.

14   Applicants with an affidavit still had to wait for their immigration quota number to come up. The Knoepflmachers would have had to wait another year to come to the United States, so they elected to go to Bolivia where a job was awaiting Georg.

more than other such organizations, apparently because, being located at the other end of the continent, they are less in demand.

Should I add the habitual family report? Right now that seems rather crazy, when I reflect that at least one letter already on its way to you contains information that has already become outdated. Your mother, Steffi,[15] and the children are fine, thank God. They received two letters from you today. That Herman moved in with Ossi you already know from Mama Erna. Hedy[16] writes from Rome that she may have a chance to emigrate to England and Uruguay. Franz W. has his permit, but had to postpone his departure, although his ship won't leave until December. I just learned from Hella a few hours ago that there have been new problems with the transference of the E. W. D. primarily because of the price involved.

Edith and Fred[17] are healthy, though dejected; Hans has rallied thanks to your affidavit; Egon seems at peace in Zagreb; my brother-in-law[18] has reached his destination[19] and wrote while on his way there from Haifa.

And every one else is sending wires all over the world in the hope that someone out there can help them emigrate. But it wasn't this psychosis, believe me, that led me to wire you; it was simply the need to steer towards the only visible source of light that you yourselves have come to appreciate.

The curriculum vitae I had planned to enclose will go out in the next mail, since I did not want to delay this letter any further, already much interrupted.

Do not be mad at me!
With steadfast love, your,
Georg

---

15   Steffi: Rudy's sister, husband, Herman. Ossi, Oscar, married to Rudy's sister, Minka.
16   Hedy Planer, a cousin of Rudy.
17   Georg's sister and brother-in-law
18   Fritz Weiss
19   Syria

Rudy-Boy

Your telegram arrived last evening. All three of us bawled, because it came at exactly the right time to calm our badly strained nerves. I immediately wired you back to convey in far too limited words the depth of our gratitude and I am writing now again to say what Hildusch[20] advised against saying in a telegram: May the eternal God reward you and your dear ones for what you have done for us! The refusal of Portugal came today; imagine how we would have otherwise received such news! On the other hand, Eva and Fritz[21] had good news today. Special greetings from your respective mothers, both have greatly welcomed your great deed, stirred both by kindness and by the kindling of their own hopes.

Hugging you in behalf of all of us, your,
Georg,

---

20   Hilda Knoepflmacher, Georg's wife
21   Eva and Fred [Fritz] Markus were Rudy's niece and nephew. Teenagers, they came to Chicago and were part of the Weiner household until their parents were able to establish a home.

2 December 1938 Vienna

From Georg Knoepflmacher

Dearest Käthe!

Your letter of November 18 has deeply moved us in its reassertion of our steadfast bonds. But I cannot avoid reproaching myself that despite the fears I mentioned in my last letter, I may have plunged you into an improper panic. I therefore must ask myself whether, given your account of its reception, my telegram might not have led you to offer a gift that you might have otherwise have chosen to bestow on someone else. Still, I should say in my defense that there actually was only a hair's breadth separating your surmise from actuality. Moreover, factors (which cannot be described here in full detail) compelled me to follow the advice of friends and to send you a telegram instead of the letter I had planned. So please do not be angry and believe me that I had no intention to overwhelm you or even to mislead you. The fact remains that the affidavit now offers a foundation for all our plans for the future. It would be better, I think, to send it to us at Margaretenstrasse 82, so that we can immediately have it photo-copied. Your previous practice guarantees that it will go off in ship-shape completion. Since we did not register[22] until last July, our quota-turn would not come until April to June, unless there is some truth in rumors that earlier immigration dates might be granted. Our task thus would be to bridge the interval. I thus welcomed the offer of my Dutch correspondents to work for them for three months in Peru. But these people seem insincere; they have delayed all local contractors with mere promises and increasingly reveal themselves in the worst way as exploiters of the current situation. I have also explored possibilities in Palestine and England, and am considering a tourist visa for ancient Cyprus and other potential interim solutions. As I wrote to Mr. Klein (I enclose a carbon copy since you, who know German, will better understand my English than he can), I feel

---

22   At the American Embassy

hopeful about eventually succeeding in the U. S. construction business. We[23] had already decided to test the suitability of our specialties for an American market. I imagine that pylons and reinforced concrete structures, which had always been profitable here, would also be of interest there. Similarly, a connection with Hans Wottitz also has found work and prospects in New York and may offer an opportunity. Please allow me to enclose a copy of my curriculum vitae just in case that you may find a need for it at some time.

Everyone in your family, thank God, seems healthy again and confident. I visited your mother the day before yesterday and met Emil there. We naturally spoke at great length about Kagran. Your mother is an extraordinary woman, full of kindness, intelligence, and determination. Besides the Oppenheimers, Edith has obtained an affidavit, so that if the Australian plans prove unrealizable—despite the truly generous offers from their sponsors, it might be possible to expand the American family, as I fervently hope. Hedi too, received an affidavit, but also has obtained a visa for Uruguay, which would allow her an earlier departure from Rome. Mr. Klein's opinion fully chimes with mine. But today this remains the only available option since only it builds on good will and only it can give our children a start that may lead to a fail-safe and permanent resolution.

Hella, too, finds herself at the same juncture and Viktor eagerly awaits the result of his visa processing. The day before yesterday, Hella asked me for Edith's address, apparently a good sign.

Exceptional good news, thank God, can be reported about Herman, who seems unchanged and has good reasons to be satisfied. Franz W. already wrote from London, Walter S. received his landing certificate for Palestine today; my brother-in-law Fritz was able to obtain a visa for Palestine and Cyprus, so that he can now continue his business trip through this region with a permanent end in sight.

Uli, about whom you inquired, dear Käthe, is, heaven be specially thanked, hearty, well behaved, and joyous. If you haven't already heard this from other sources, it may amuse you to find out how he cheered us after our little weeping bout upon receiving the affidavit.

---

23   Refers to Georg's former director, a former business competitor, and himself.

Before going to sleep, he suddenly said: "If we move to America, I'll be able to marry 'Lieserl.' And then we'll tell Hans everything." Hilda asked: "Who is Hans, then?" Uli: "That will be our son!" — Amen.

In deep love for all four of you, greetings from

Your faithful Georg

Handwritten addition to the above from Hilda Knoepflmacher

Dearest Käthe!

I am very happy that all your assumptions have now proved correct. Look at the success that these assumptions led to; that success is our only source of hope for the future. In that sense you seem to achieve the intuitive feeling of satisfaction that you would get from a blessing spoken during an interment. Even though I didn't sign the telegram, it turns out that I was its instigator. Please rest assured that we are far more grateful than before, and that we found it too difficult to express our thoughts in a letter.

I am including an old photograph that was taken last winter in Reichenau.

Heartiest greetings and kisses
yours .... Hilda

Erna and Hans in Kagran

Erna's Transit Pass - issued by the German
government after it annexed Austria.
All Jewish women were required to add the
middle name of 'Sara.' All men had to add 'Israel.'

PART TWO

1940 – 1945 *Shanghai*

In November 1940 Hans and Erna left Vienna for Berlin. They went by train from Berlin to Moscow, and from Moscow to Vladivostok aboard the Trans-Siberian Railway. Then they took a ship to Japan, and another ship to Shanghai.[24]

The following letters were written in 1941. On 7 December 1941 the war in the Pacific began with the bombing of Pearl Harbor. There were no more letters until the war ended in 1945. The International Red Cross would convey twenty-five-word postcards between families once every three months. They could contain only news of a "personal nature." In addition, the Mayers were able to send news occasionally via travelers from Shanghai.

Letters and cards were written alternately to Gusti and Käthe, who would share them with nearby relatives and then send them to each other. The present selection was saved by Käthe.

---

24   Thousands of Austrian Jews were saved by the Chinese consul-general in Vienna, Ho Feng Shan, who issued visas (transit passes) during 1938–1940 against the orders of his superior, the Chinese ambassador in Berlin, Chen Jie. Wikipedia, Shanghai Ghetto

4 November 1941
From Erna

My dear ones all,

Your dear letter dated 2 October arrived already on 29 October; we cannot tell you how much we have enjoyed your good news. May the dear Lord only bestow good things on us so that we can wait calmly until it will be our turn. It seems easier to wait for good news. We are delighted to know that you, dear Emil, have been at your destination for the past four weeks and have achieved some happiness and satisfaction; that you have found suitable living quarters so that you can reestablish yourself again.

Dear Gusti, we already have enough of the nice landscape pictures that one likes to take. Yesterday we visited Mrs. Sinai who is still having problems with her emigration plans. She had an appointment at the American consulate to pick up her visa before making her travel arrangements. But now she has to do some bank transactions; when she arrived at the consulate they had to send a cable to Washington to get her a new visa number for November. She is to return to the consulate on Friday to resolve this visa problem. If everything is cleared up then she can leave aboard the President Coolidge liner on November 21 and then deliver our warmest regards in person. She plans to visit us next Saturday to inspect our new apartment and for a long schmooze so that she can tell you all about us. In addition, we have also invited a couple by the name of Felix. I will also keep an eye on the Josephs to see how far they have progressed in their emigration plans.

Regrettably, right now there are no direct ships going to the United States; instead people have to change ships in Manila. The trip from Manila (plus the extra expenses) costs about four hundred U.S. dollars, a pretty substantial amount.[25] But if we just plan for such a trip in the immediate future we won't complain so much. I

25    $400 would be about $5,600 in 2007

know that we all want to do that and hope to lessen the burden on you a little bit.

Our new apartment is very nice. On Sunday we were only ten people here. The Kollmanns arrived late and then stayed for supper. Now our home has become another popular stopping place for an excursion, just like Kagran. Of course, I cannot really fuss since the inflation here is terrible. Currently, one U.S. dollar is worth about forty Shanghai dollars. For example, a small can of condensed milk costs $2.60; a pound of sugar or flour costs $1.30[26]—thus nothing is cheap now. I am not complaining about our circumstances, but it is a mystery to me how the local population survives with these prices. Similarly, postage costs have just doubled. We also know that you pass on our letters. Therefore we will not write separately to the Blochs, or to the Neubauers.[27] We do expect to hear soon about an addition to their family. We hope that everything will proceed smoothly with them, and hope for some news very soon. We also hope that dear Lore and her children are doing well. We still have unending worries about all of the dear people back in the old country.

We just read yesterday that the Nazis are seizing all Jewish properties. So now we really cannot figure out how my sisters can continue to exist there. Now they are completely alone. We just cannot talk about their situation; this state of things has lasted for a long time and they have never had much money. Regrettably, none of our deliberations can do a bit of good for them, nor can we truly help them. And to our sorrow, we cannot foresee an end to their suffering. I have been telling everybody that emigration is not a simple matter for young people, but it becomes a hopeless problem for people of our age. It is a very rare case when an older person can restart a career successfully. We do complain and cannot save any money, but we are able to stint on ourselves. We know that you are willing to do this too. Father could have had a low-level position in a large

---

26   These amounts are in Shanghai dollars.

27   Fred and Richard Neubauer were distant relatives of the Mayers and childhood friends of Emil Glauber from Tachau. They settled in New York and were lifelong friends.

fabric factory, for an annual salary of about $250 to $300.[28] But this firm is located at the end of Hongkew. He would have had to spend two dollars for the fare, in addition to leaving at 7 a.m. Therefore I talked him out of this job because of his age. Sooner or later the climate also gets in the way. I am very happy that we are healthy and therefore want to avoid any experiments. We still have not withdrawn money, since we would have to accept the official exchange rate of 18.60 Shanghai dollars per U.S. dollar. Mrs. Sinai has received a check from her husband—this money seems to be subject to a better exchange rate. But this doesn't mean that we need money. We still have enough here; all I'm saying is that I only hope we have enough to leave Shanghai when our turn comes. But in that case we would ask for money if it were feasible.

---

28    $250 would be about $3,500 in 2007 using the consumer price index.
James R. Ross in Escape to Shanghai "The European Jewish refugees ...were among the lowest-paid workers in Shanghai. ...One of the best jobs available was with an egg dealer, whose ten employees worked for twelve hours a day and had Sundays off, earning less than $3 a week...Jewish night watchmen earned 25 to 30 cents a night, about a quarter of what Sikh watchmen earned for the same work."

7 November 1941   Shanghai

From Hans Mayer

My dears,

I feel certain that the next airmail letter will precede this letter. After all, now nobody knows how long it will take a letter to reach its destination. Since we want to write you as often as possible, we sometimes use surface mail. There is the additional reason due to the fact that as of 2 November the postage rate was doubled. We are very curious about a report about you, dear Emil.[29] But first we anticipate getting news about you, dear Guckerl, since Emil will be too busy to write, particularly since first he will have to handle his own letters by himself. He will be plenty busy with writing his letters even if he uses carbon copies. We hope that he is not disappointed with his job and he'll get used to his new environment. We were very delighted with your airmail letter of 7 October that arrived on the twenty-seventh. We wish that the good Lord will keep all of you in good health, and you will be able to send us reports telling us that you are satisfied with your lives even though obviously many things remain not so satisfactory. One cannot achieve perfection in everything as you picture it in your imagination. If you consider all the misfortune in the world, we just cannot be dissatisfied and thank the good Lord.

Now we hope that the next several letters will also contain satisfactory news about dear Mawei's[30] fate—she is really very close to our hearts. *Allewei*,[31] she has made the boat trip to Cuba and withstood the stress. Obviously, we are extremely worried about Emma, Clara, and especially Paula,[32] since we have had no direct correspondence from

29   Emil had been offered a job in Cleveland by his former employer. The family lived there for three years.
30   Mawei: Bertha Weiner, Rudy's mother. Erna later refers to Emil Glauber's mother as Maglau, and Susi Juer Glauber's mother as Maju.
31   Yiddish - God willing
32   Clara and Paula were Erna's sisters. Clara had been writing weekly to Erna from Vienna. Her last letter was dated October 4, 1941. Erna learned later that Clara had been deported to Poland on October 15, 1941. Emma was Hans' sister. The fate of Emma and Paula is unknown.

them, and we have heard that all Jewish properties have been seized. We are very afraid that they may be in dire need—God forbid; we are truly helpless and cannot provide any help to them from here.

It was very interesting to hear what you, dear Gucki, wrote us about dear Emil's replacement. I still remember him as a beginner in our business who had been assigned to work for you. It is also our understanding that Mr. Heller feels that he doesn't have business know-how for his role, and therefore will remain in his current assignment. This is also very important because the Schwomers are also still working there. I'll be very curious how these people will be able to stay. I was also very pleased with the decency exhibited by Emil's boss, at least from a moral point of view. That really seems to be some testimony to Emil's diligence, effectiveness in business, and honesty. When you criticize my poor judgment with respect to financial matters, you are probably correct; but here one loses the ability to judge things properly. But if your American dollar is worth as much as here, then one can earn a fortune within a very short time.

When your most recent letter arrived we had already moved into our new quarters. Mrs. Sinai is kind enough to take these letters with her, and then certainly you will have heard about how we are doing physically, as well as how we are living here. Yesterday she visited us with her sister-in-law and cousin; we really enjoyed their visit. It was also a particular pleasure to let them observe with their own eyes how we are living here. Then they can report to you directly; we don't doubt the fact that you all will agree with their observations of our life here. Yesterday, in addition to these three ladies, the Kollmanns also arrived for *jause*.[33] A little later Hans Klinger came to us for supper; the Kollmanns also stayed. So you can see that nothing much has changed in our daily lives. Klinger will be joining us again on Wednesday. After supper we three are supposed to go to the movies to see *Mrs. Hamilton*. Of course, we are trying to maintain a normal life, but our worries about our loved ones keep us up day and night. Even though we would like to help each of them, we just can't go against the cruelties of fate. So far we have not withdrawn your second transmission of US $125 since we receive only 18.60 Shanghai

33   Afternoon coffee

dollars per U.S. dollar; actually we should get 40 to 42 Shanghai dollars for each U.S. dollar. If I leave the money at American Express until the end of the month and don't get a better exchange rate, then I will return the money. It makes no sense to waste money. After all, you don't earn your money so easily. Based on our ability to forecast the future, we expect to stay here for another one and a half to two years. Therefore I am trying to figure out a better way to proceed. We also need to consider the travel costs. Lord knows if and when that option will become a reality. If this event does occur in the near future, we don't know how to cover those expenses. So that will become a real problem whose solution I cannot fathom right now. But one cannot worry about every possibility—after all we tend to get smarter advice as time passes. Actually, so far the good Lord always has been looking out for us. Therefore I will thank the Lord and trust the Lord. As far as I am concerned personally, you can see how well I am doing, as well as from what Mrs. Sinai told you. As your mother reported, I could have a job and make more money, but that would involve about one and a half hours of walking and transportation time from here; furthermore, I would be spending one half of my salary on commuting. Therefore I have decided to forget about this particular job at this time; perhaps a better job will become available in the future.

I have been very surprised what you, dear Gucki, have written about Lore.[34] I am very sorry that *das schatzerl*[35] is suffering from so many internal conflicts; hopefully, that situation will end very soon. After all, the children have been put through several significant changes in their schools and thus through many different educational experiences. Obviously, this has not been easy for them. Hopefully, you, dear Gucki, will have fortitude and patience so that *das schatzerl* will not have to suffer excessively from her parents' nervousness. It is very important to understand all of this; you can rightfully say that your father can easily tell you what to do. We cannot always help you, but only offer advice. Furthermore, we are too far removed from the thought processes of the younger generation.

---

34   Eleanor Glauber, Gusti's daughter
35   A term of endearment, literally dear little treasure. .

We hope that you are not too worried about the long time intervals between letters. But we seem to have found a wonderful *postillion d'amour*[36] so our letters may reach you faster than through the mail.

Your report about Käthe's connections sounds like a fairy tale. Dear Rudy, I can only tell you that some prophetess seems to be right. But as all of you can understand, we have not relied on her predictions. Our new apartment has been furnished as a permanent home, that is, to be nice and comfortable so that we needn't be ashamed to receive guests. That should also offer you the pleasure of recognizing that we truly appreciate your sacrifices and worrying. As much as possible, we would like to spare you any worries about our well being. We are delighted to hear good news about your children. When we compare the newest photos with the earlier ones, we can see immediately that they are growing up. We'd be unable to recognize them.

How are the cousins doing, Rosette[37] for instance? Dear Käthe, are you getting along with her? How is the gentleman who gave us our affidavit? Has he moved back to Chicago? Shouldn't we write him again? How are your old friends doing? This week we met Mr. Joseph; they plan to visit us later this week. Are you still in touch with their children? We are attaching some more letters for some other people—please be good enough to forward them. Apparently they reach their intended recipients more quickly than if we mailed them directly. We also don't know really which of them got our letters, or which ones. Except for the letters you have written, for several months we have not heard directly from Emma, Mawei, Paula, or other surviving relatives. We hope that everything at the Blochs is normal by now; we would love to hear from them and the Rosensteins[38] with lots of details. Please send my warmest regards to the Neubauers. I love to receive newsy letters from them.

Heartiest kisses to you all, your Father

---

36   A special delivery person who does it for love

37   Rosette Hirsch was a distant cousin of Rudy. She was a sponsor of the family. She and her son Morris met the Weiner family at their ship arrival in New York, drove them to Chicago and helped them settle.

38   Ernst and Trude Rosenstein, first cousins of Käthe. They settled in San Francisco.

10 November 1941 Shanghai

From Erna

To all of my very dear ones,

Sometimes it becomes advantageous not to rush into writing letters too often. So the time is ripe now to send this letter with Mrs. Sinai who is kind enough to take a few things with her. I am truly not envious of her. After all, she has not seen her husband and son for three years—a very long time. We hope that everything will work out smoothly for her. On Wednesday we plan to wave good-bye to her from the pier. She is still quite worried if she can arrange her trip to Manila. But since she has made her plans so carefully up to now we hope that everything will work out for her. She will tell you all about us; last Saturday she was here with her sister-in-law and cousin to inspect our new apartment. Since she had also seen our old home she will be able to confirm that we actually made a change for the better. So now it looks like it did in Hitzing.[39] We have become very uppity: on Friday we bought an old hand-knotted carpet, 3 by 3 yards in size, so that we can be warm in the wintertime. It cost us two hundred fifty Shanghai dollars, while one U.S. dollar is equivalent to forty Shanghai dollars—we hope that you won't be mad at us for wasting money. We assume that this rug will stay here with our household goods. When it comes to that point, we will be happy to lose some of our possessions. As before, we keep on having lots of company. Yesterday we were at the Rittermanns. While we were gone, Mrs. Bleier and Leo Gewitsch tried to visit us. You might say that we seem to be victims of popularity. That's just too bad. But at least time passes so that we can spend our time on our emigration plans as during last year. Probably all the transient residents here have had the very same experience. This seems quite acceptable during the daytime hours, but we spend many evening and sleeping hours worrying about these problems. Whenever we hear some bad

---

39   The family's summer place in the 13th district of Vienna.

news, we tend to believe it. Mrs. Else is very nice. She plans to bring the tuxedo sent to me by Maglau so that Emil can use it. She also left me with three sheep's wool outfits. If practical, I'd like to send Käthe and Gusti some housedresses. This afternoon I am planning to go with Mrs. Rittermann to look at these clothes. Perhaps I'll find what I am looking for. I think that you, dear Emil, may find an occasion to wear this tuxedo. We continue to do well. My oil stove seems to work quite well. In fact, last week I baked a Gugelhupf[40] in that oven—I was really proud of myself. Do I have troubles? Of course, the Lord knows that I have lots of troubles; I would love to change our circumstances, to our regret there seems to be no way to make a change

As usual, the Kollmanns were with us on Saturday; on Thursday we go over to their home to have supper with them. Naturally, we continue to study English, but instinctively I feel that I am at a dead spot. Nevertheless I am not giving up. A little bit does get stuck in my head. But we aren't going to start speaking English until we are really forced to do so. In Shanghai we can usually get along in German.

Now we are really curious how you, dear Emil, like Cleveland, and what your prospects are for finding living quarters. The children are bound to suffer from this change. From the bottom of my heart I wish for you that you have found a permanent home, in spite of the uproar caused by the relocation. *Allewei*, it will be very nice if you can stay there. The Josephs have made no progress in their emigration plans. That is just not a simple situation. I cannot imagine what the children look like. They have all grown up, and Lieserl has also started to go to school! So we seem to have lost a lot of opportunities to watch the children's progress that we would have loved to enjoy, together with you. But we are not complaining, because we were spared from many worse things. So we'll continue to wait and keep up our hopes. Dear Gusti, I am sure you are not lacking for things to do; I wish I could take some of the load off your shoulders. I am rotting away here. After all, all I am doing here is a little cooking

---

40   A cake of yeast dough with raisins and almonds baked in a bundt pan.

and shopping. We do have an amah here that washes the dishes and takes care of the laundry for small items. I think that I'll be unable to afford her in the future. Dear Käterl, how are your patients doing? I hope that they'll recover their health and that your massage therapy will really help them; but all that will take some time. If you keep on performing this massage therapy, you probably will have to pass an examination. I am convinced that anything you start, you'll also complete successfully. We hope that Oscar[41] has found a new job. It is very sad to find out that you can be laid off so easily over there. They just leave you dangling in midair. But now business seems to be doing well, and he should get another job very soon. How is Ruth[42] doing? Is she working as a hat maker? Everyone needs to struggle in their everyday lives, but hopefully each of us will remain healthy, and build up a new career, thanks be to God. The Rittermanns would like to know how Hans Bettelheim is doing; he used to be Hans Schnitzer's business partner. Perhaps you can ask him since you seem to be in touch with him by letter. I am very sorry that nobody is getting any mail from us in the old country. We seem to have gotten all of their mail. It has been a long time since we have received any mail from Paula, as well as from Maglau. May the good Lord protect both of them. We are very lonesome for all of them. Mrs. Sinai is a very capable person with lots of common sense who will tell you everything of interest to you.

Now good-bye to you all, our dear ones, particularly the little one.

Heartiest kisses from your Mother

---

41   The brother-in-law of Rudy, married to Hermine (Minka). He had been a co-manager of the E.W.D.

42   Daughter of Oscar and Minka. She graduated from Northwestern University in Chicago and became a chemist, and later a librarian in Minneapolis.

21 November 1941   Shanghai

From Erna

My dear Blochs[43] and Rosensteins,

We were really delighted to receive your dear letter, so now we want to respond to you in a hurry. Since we are not using airmail, it may take some time for this letter to reach you. Since the New Year is imminent, please accept my sincerest wishes now for a Happy New Year for 1942. I just don't want to waste too many words. Hopefully, you will be able to settle down for many more years and enjoy your children and grandchildren. Probably the children will be very happy; we would be overjoyed to receive a little picture of them. I am delighted to hear that you, dear Agnes, have gotten used to things by now, and that you are gaining some weight as you told us. That surely should benefit your nerves. We cannot say the same here; people tend to blame that on the local climate.

Up to now, the climate has not really bothered me, or dear Hans. And I am not shedding any tears about my weight loss. We have been doing well, and as I have been saying, we are not really complaining about our situation when we think of all the others who are still in our old country. You are absolutely right that we are so very happy that dear Emil is now so well situated. Whenever I talk to people about him, I get to hoping that we will see one another again. But will that happen? When talking to one another, we always seem to hear about people who have made some progress in their emigration plans, but we are not among them. We still hope that we will get to that point. In the meantime we have bought secondhand furniture. In my wildest dreams I never imagined that I would be furnishing an apartment in Shanghai. So everything turns out different than we had planned originally. But when we are waiting for something then it is only temporary—perhaps the future change will occur sooner. I am delighted that you have started to acquire new friends. Lots of

___

43   Agnes and Gustav Bloch. Agnes was Hans's sister.

things are going on here so that our week is always busy. We have to keep ourselves occupied; if we were always ruminating about our sad fate the time would not pass any faster. Now it has been almost one year since our arrival here in Shanghai; in all honesty I have to admit that time has passed quickly, in exemplary fashion. After all we always seem to remember the past; so we thank the good Lord that at least we are here now. And now we feel much closer to our children. We are also very happy to know that Mawei has escaped the hell;[44] she'll be able to tell many stories. We hope that she can reach her final destination very soon. But the Lord has not made that very easy.

We have had no direct news from the Rosensteins. We hope that you, dear Trude, are completely healthy again, and that you are satisfied with your caregiver; it normally isn't very easy to find a replacement. I am very sorry for you, dear Ernst, that you have been unable to find a job in your specialty. I imagined that that task would be much easier. But normally that task rarely turns out to be easy. It also seems that your brother will have no chance to join you. At least we hope that you are hearing good things from him and that his mother is feeling reasonably healthy. Yesterday we had supper at the Kollmanns. They served us "Chinese chow" that we ate in Chinese style, with chopsticks. Here people really like to eat that way. Occasionally we go to Chinese restaurants. Sometimes people also invite us to such restaurant meals. I just remembered that you, my dear, will have a birthday tomorrow. There should be a nice birthday cake; I hope that all your wishes come true.

Stay well; send warmest regards to the Felixes, to the Rosensteins, and anyone else.

Many kisses yours, Mother

Please forward the enclosed letter to the Neubauers and to Rose Klinger-Taussig. Many thanks.

---

44   Mawei, Rudy's mother, went by ship to Cuba before entering the United States. She then lived in Chicago with the Weiner family. She died in Oakland, California in 1961.

21 November 1941 Shanghai

From Hans Mayer to Gustav Bloch, Palo Alto, California

My dear ones,

A few days ago, the mailman delivered two letters to us from you, and our dear children, dated October 4 and October 15. We are delighted to know that, thanks be to God, all of you are in good health. We can really understand that you, dear Gustav, are finding it very hard to find a suitable job. But as is obvious from your letters, at least you seem to be able to do some translations. Even though you may not earn very much money, you should consider this income as more than pocket money. The effort will keep you busy, as well as offer you a chance to improve the language talents that you possess already. But I lack all those opportunities here. I could have found a good job by now if I had a better knowledge of English. There always seems to be an obstacle: either my age or my lack of knowing the English language. Over time, I have gotten used to all the rejections, but there is nothing else for me to do. One has to suffer through so many adversities and accept them patiently, but we tend to omit these trivial things from our conversations and correspondence. Of course, our chances for emigrating from here are completely uncertain in view of the current situation.

Tomorrow a few people are leaving who have already received their visas. They are supposed to deliver greetings to our children in person, and perhaps even some letters if there are no constraints. Only the Almighty can predict what the future will bring. We have always trusted in the Lord in the past, and plan to do the same in the future. Actually, we are doing quite well, with the exception of various problem issues that are just beyond help. As usual, we have lots of company, just for *schmoozing*. That occupies our time, instead of always worrying to no avail. In fact, I even have a steady card game that I could schedule even more frequently, but I don't seem to have that much time. First of all, I have to do occasional errands; since they tend to be far away they chew up the time very quickly. Then I also have to perform certain household tasks that usually turn out to be entirely unsuccessful. So we normally end up going to bed no earlier than 11:30 p.m. or midnight. Erna gets up between 6 and 7 a.m., and I get up a half hour later. So you can see that we really lead fairly stressful lives, and so far we have not been bored.

I am delighted that you can talk to fellow Austrians—it is easier to talk to them than to Germans. We have the same experience here, where we meet many people from Germany—they seem to be very nice and well behaved, but we can get along with fellow Austrians far better. Our living quarters are very nice; we have sublet a very nice and bright room that faces south so that we cannot really complain. Actually, as emigrants we really are living exceptionally well, almost in the European style. But if I were to write a more realistic report about our lives here, you would see how our living habits have changed.[45] I need to stress that our lifestyle here is not really worse than previously, but thanks be to God we are still able to adjust to life here. Actually, the local climate is incomparably better than we had been told. It was very wrong for the first immigrants here to describe the local climate so cruelly. That wrong impression convinced many prospective immigrants to accept a far worse and catastrophic fate by avoiding Shanghai as a destination, and, instead, staying behind in their home communities. Actually, in comparison, staying here is close to being in paradise. *Allewei*, our Emma, Mawei, and many of our friends and relatives did exactly that. We also cannot help worrying that Clara, Paula, etc., have done the very same thing.[46] At the same time the exchange of letters between us and them now has become rarer.

We are very happy—thanks be to God—that by now dear Emil has secured a position commensurate with his talents and capabilities.

---

45   James Ross describes conditions in Shanghai in Escape to Shanghai: "stifling humidity in summer and heavy rains that would flood the streets in October…Dozens of Chinese froze to death on the streets during the cold winter months….The Europeans were particularly vulnerable to lethal strains of dysentery—unheard of in Europe—which killed hundreds of them." p. 65–66

46   Erna did not know whether her sisters and Mawei had escaped from Austria since they were still in Vienna when she left.

The children will have to get used to residing farther away, but nobody can have everything they want.[47] Thanks be to God that dear Lore is doing well again, that eliminates a major worry. We cannot appreciate good health; Nestroy[48] wrote that there are many illnesses, but only one healthy state. May God keep all our loved ones in good health; then with God's help everything will turn out well. I am delighted that the Rosensteins are doing well again, but I would be even more pleased if I heard from them directly. It seems amazing that I hear only the most minimal news about Sigmund and Bertha, as well as from their sons. Have you heard if Dr. Paul Engel, Seppl's husband[49] was in Chicago? He was supposed to contact our children there several weeks ago, but we have not heard anything more. Since Olga's departure we have not heard anything about her or her children. I can readily imagine that Felix is extremely busy. But I believe that his children will offer him an opportunity to relax. Hopefully, he will spend his vacation resting, so that he can return with renewed strength. I would also be very interested to find out if he has achieved some material gain from his endeavors. Here I am not referring to his scientific papers, but his success in applying his theoretical concepts to some practical use. So I am still very curious how his very hard work, knowledge, and diligence will pay off in a practical sense.[50] Did Felix give up his car? After all, that car was his hobby! If you meet the Hellers please convey our warmest regards to his wife and him.

Now I want to end this letter. I want to send my warmest regards to you, to your children, and to your grandchildren. I hope that you will be able to continue reporting good news about them.

Heartiest kisses, yours, Hans

---

47   The Glauber family moved from Aurora, Illinois to Cleveland when Emil was offered a job designing textile factories. In Aurora they had been near the Weiner family in Chicago.

48   The Austrian poet Johann Nestroy

49   Seppl Engel was a distant cousin of Käthe. The Engels settled in Quito, Ecuador.

50   Felix Bloch received the Nobel Prize in Physics in 1954.

The following letter, unlike the others, which were translated from the German, was written in English by Hans Mayer. Dated September 8, 1942, it is the first letter since Pearl Harbor—December 7, 1941. The letter is included as it was written.

8 September 1942 Shanghai

Our dearest all!

Through the kindness of our landlady, is one other lady so kind to take along this letter. I will hope that you get shortly this news. We are really healthy and you must not have fear for us. We have all the things which need to us. We have a great number of good friends what take care of us. Under [the aegis of] the Engel, Ing. Schwarz, Kardos, Kolls. With Kolls are always one or two times the week together. Hans Klinger live with us in the same building and take the breakfast and supper every day by us. He is one of the best. Our greatest care are you all, the grandchildren, the sisters, your parents, dear Emil and your mother dear Rudy. We are since nearly one year without every news. We think always by all our dears. God help that we can see us again in not too long time.

But it is necessary to have very much patience. The summer is very long and more hot than the last but we will hope that we are again healthy. We had so much to ask for so long. We had no news from you and we will pray to God that you are all, including the children, healthy. Yesterday Lore had birthday and we have much to think on her. We think she had a nice party and had a great number of presents. With great pleasure we were also been at this party. Sorry that this is not possible. We will hope that we will have one time the opportunity to be by all birthdays from our dears.

We will make the attempt also to write to Felix and hope that any news came to you. Our thoughts are always by you and we will be happy to hear from you.

Many heartiness kisses your father and mother. Hans Mayer

[Handwritten] in love your mother

TELEGRAM from HICEM[51]
6 August 1943 Lisbon

To Heinrich Mayer, Shanghai
[In English] Herbert and Edith Gutwillig have been very glad when receiving news from him; they are doing well and make a living. Gusti and Käthe and their families are quite content. They are worried about Mr. Mayer. He may write to them through Messrs Niepoort, Av. Dos Aliados, Oporto.

On the reverse:
From Heinrich Mayer
Messrs Niepoort Av. Dos Aliados, Oporto
[In German] Happy with the report from Gutwillig and our children. We are in good health. I have a job and some earnings and what is missing we get from Engel and Huber. Please thank them. We live at Ing. Schwarz with Kollmanns and friends. We get along with all. It is not necessary to worry about us. Our longing for all is very great.
Kisses—Parents.
Shanghai 25 November 1943
1106 Point Road

---

51   HICEM is an acronym for three agencies aiding Jewish emigration: HIAS- Hebrew Sheltering and Immigration Society, ICA – Jewish Colonization Association and Emigdirect

Bubbling Well Lane (in 2009)

Hongkew Hutong (in 2009)

RED CROSS LETTERS

The American and Swiss Red Cross transmitted inquiry letters between families during the years when there was no mail between China and the United States. The writers were allowed "not more than 25 words, family news of strictly personal character." These letters had to be written in the Red Cross offices on postal cards. They are all in English. The reply was written on the reverse side and received many months later.

Inquirer: Gustav Bloch   Palo Alto, California   March 30, 1942

We all Californians. All is well. So are Weiners and Glaubers as we heard by personal visitor. We hope the best for you all. Kisses Agnes

Reply: Heinrich Mayer Shanghai November 30, 1942

Happy to get good news from you and our children. We are well also are Kolls. We get what we need from Engel. Many kisses in great love. Erna & Hans Mayer

---

Inquirer: Emil Glauber, Cleveland. Ohio. April 20, 1942
Everybody happy and fine. Satisfied with job. Children doing nicely. Good news from relatives. Burgers very kind, have nice home. Answer same way. Emil and Gusti
Reply: Heinrich Mayer, Shanghai, December 25, 1942
Happy to hear good news. We are healthy and earn with baking beugel. Engel take care for us. We are afraid for relatives. We will hope to see us again. Many kisses. Your Mother and Father

---

Inquirer: Käthe and Rudolph Weiner, Chicago, Illinois, March 24, 1943
Dear Parents: Received your messages last August. All of us including Rudy's Mother who lives with us are in best health and busy. See Glaubers frequently. Love
Reply: "parents" Shanghai November 24, 1943
Dearest all! Happy with letter we are healthy have good friends and a good room. Father has good job and what we need we get from Engelhuber.[52] Longing for you all.
Kisses Parents

---

52   Refers to the Engel and the Huber families.

Inquirer: Heinrich Mayer, Shanghai, April 5, 1943

Our dearest. Are sorry that without any letter from you, and afraid. We hope you all healthy and have your job. For us have no care. Kisses Heinrich Mayer

Reply Käthe and Rudy Weiner, Chicago, Ilinois, February 26, 1944

Dearest Mother and Father: Received your good Red Cross news. Will never forget kindness of your friends. We all working. Rudy's mother housekeeper for us.

Your loving children, Käthe and Rudy

Inquirer Heinrich Mayer September 27, 1943

Are well. Father has a job. Otherwise Engelhuber cares for us. Please recognize this. Unfortunately without any report. Hope you are well and satisfied. God willing soon we'll meet again.

Reply: Käthe & Rudy Weiner, Chicago, Illinois, May 4, 1944

Happy with your messages. We will never forget Engelhubers kindness. Here all healthy, happy but longing and praying for you. Stay well. All our love

Inquirer: Heinrich Mayer, Shanghai, February 29, 1944

Without your message hope you are well also we are. Father earn and Engelhuber take again care for us. Longing is great also for sisters and friends. Love, parents. Erna Mayer

Reply: Rudy and Käthe Weiner, Chicago, Illinois, October 27, 1944

Happy with your frequent news. Hope you stay well. Will never forget kindness of your friends. We all in best of health, happy, longing for you, Much love, Rudy & Käthe Weiner

Erna Mayer, Shanghai, February 27, 1945

Dearest! Unhappy to inform you that poor father died the 23 February after ten weeks very hard disease. He went to sleep and we must wish him the peace. Love, Mutter

Attached to the reverse of this card

THE ATTACHED MESSAGE HAS BEEN HELD BY THE OFFICE OF CENSORSHIP AND JUST RELEASED TO THE AMERICAN RED CROSS. MAIL SERVICE IS NOW OPEN TO CHINA. KEEP THIS MESSAGE, THEREFORE, AND REPLY BY LETTER THROUGH REGULAR MAILS.

AMERICAN RED CROSS

FOREIGN SERVICE DEPARTMENT

Dated: DEC 17 1945

Heinrich Mayer
Shanghai Identification Card

Liesl, Henry, George, Eleanor Chicago 1940

PART THREE

1945–1946 *After the War*

Victory in Europe was declared on 7 and 8 May 1945. Japan surrendered between 14 August and 2 September 1945 and very soon withdrew from Shanghai. By 14 June 1945, the mail channels between China and the United States were open, and Erna sent her first long letter, recounting the events between November 1941 and June 1945.

She wrote of the Proclamation of 1943, which required the stateless refugees in Shanghai to move into the ghetto of Hongkew. She referred to the Engels and the Schwarzes. The Schwarzes had been business associates of Hans for many years before the war. Since they had been in Shanghai long before 1938, they were not required to move into Hongkew and were able to help Erna and Hans financially and in other ways.

Since she didn't know which of her letters had been received by her daughters, she repeated the story of Hans's death several times. This may have helped her in dealing with the fact of it. She was a widow at just sixty-one years of age.

Erna didn't receive the first letter of reply until 12 November 1945.

She and her daughters in the United States wrote each other weekly and she finally began to understand what had happened to her sisters and her other relatives and friends who had stayed behind in Austria and Czechoslovakia.

During the years that followed Hans's death, Erna learned to accept her new role as a widow. She was able to move back to a nicer apartment on Bubbling Well Road in the French Concession and she began to find pleasures amid her sorrows as she made plans to join the family in the United States.

14 June 1945 [53] Shanghai

From Erna

Dear children and grandchildren,

For a long time we have had the intention—just in case we are not fortunate enough to see all of you beloved relatives again—to leave you with a history of how we have loved you, just in case we could not meet you again in person. Regrettably, we never carried out this intention at an earlier time, so your dear father can no longer speak with you. I have written you repeatedly that this poor soul passed away on 23 February. During his most recent times he had no other interests except his children and grandchildren.

He first got sick on 16 December with a heart attack. He recovered fairly well from this heart attack. After about six weeks he developed pneumonia and a rib infection; that was extremely painful for him. We had the very best team of physicians: Dr. Spaniermann, Egon Kollmann, and Dr. Goldhammer. They did their humanly best for him, but in vain. He had terrible nights and did not know what was happening to him. His imagination seemed to have gone wild. The physicians said that he was accumulating fluid in his brain. During the day his mind was clear. He frequently asked me to forgive him for being nasty to me. I nursed him alone for ten weeks. His next-to-last night was so bad that we considered bringing him into the hospital. Dr. Spaniermann opposed this idea, but asked for a consultation with a neurologist. The neurologist did not arrive during the next day. Then poor father preferred to die suddenly in my arms. I had just placed him on a bedpan when he fell to one side. I moved him back and yelled for help. Nobody heard me immediately. He closed his eyes within a minute and never opened them again. What can I tell you about what happened in my mind at that moment, as well as since then? During the last night I was not allowed to watch him, but the gentlemen in our apartment complex took turns—in pairs—watching

---

53   Five weeks after VE Day

his body. Literally, I could not go on at that point. I didn't change clothes for four weeks. When morning arrived, father said, "Are you here already? Did you have something for breakfast?" I washed him and cleaned up the room. I went to the kitchen for a moment and then said I don't like the way the gentleman who is watching father looks. I sent the man away. Father died just five minutes later. I guess that Father was waiting for me so he could pass away. I am very grateful to him for allowing me to do everything for him. Dear children, don't cry for your father. He suffered a lot and very badly. So we wish for him to rest in peace. Even though this experience has been so very difficult for me. His statement, "I didn't know that dying is so very difficult," will provide a better understanding for you as to how he felt. He always expressed the desire that I should commit suicide with him. When I told him not to consider this idea, he said that the children will get over it and that the experience will pass by quickly.

He was really an old man since August 1, 1943. He had a stroke then; his right hand was always trembling and he was dragging his foot. He also had severe difficulties in maintaining his balance. But all of these medical problems seemed to have eased later on. He started to leave our apartment again and happily did errands for me. He also liked to play cards, but preferred to kibitz at home as the "lord and master." There were twenty-one people in our apartment complex, who were always very nice to us. In particular, the Kriegls (our neighbors) had many disrupted nights while father was ill. They were always ready to help us. Mr. Schwarz Brown-Boveri was always very helpful to us because of his bodily strength. Initially, we had to lift father onto the bedpan. We had to move him into a new position very often, to make him comfortable, both day and night. Everyone else was equally helpful. Otherwise, it would have been impossible for me to nurse Father at home. Obviously, I cannot tell you all the details, but our friends here have been extremely helpful. Ernst Engel and his wife were particularly good friends. Mr. Engel made it his personal concern to make life easier for poor father. He was always ready to offer sound advice when needed. May God reward him! But now, regrettably, I have the opportunity to make up for their good deeds in the past. For the past two months Mrs. Engel has been having some medical problems with her lungs. Mr. Engel asked me to help run his household with another woman helping out. I am supposed to supervise this help and to keep the household running while Mrs. Engel gets her bed rest and good food. I am very sad about this medical reason, but I am happy that I have the physical strength to help them. They are also very glad to have me at this time. They have an eighteen-year-old daughter who is attending school. She does the cooking occasionally, when she has some spare time.

In the meantime I also have the opportunity to visit father's burial place. I had him cremated with the intention of bringing his ashes with me if I am lucky enough to come to you. I just cannot bear the thought of leaving him here all alone. Will that ever happen?

I also want to point out that I am eating with the Engels. This really improves my financial situation. There have been inflationary price rises here. We have documents here that describe our local debts. I hope that eventually you will be able to clear up these debts. We have always lived modestly and never spent money on unnecessary things. In fact, Father was quite content with his life and liked the food he was served, except for the last few weeks. I have no qualms about how we spent our money here.

Now I want to tell you how we spent our years here. I will start at the point in time when our previous exchange of letters stopped. At that time we moved from our first apartment to one that was owned by a dentist (Egon's office partner). It was a very nice place to live in, but the people were so nasty to us that we got into fights with them. With the aid of Mrs. Kardos, we found another room, on Bubbling Well Road, in the same house where she lived. We rented this room from a Dutch lady, Mrs. Boeckbinder. She was very nice to us and helped us wherever she could. Regrettably, she was interned in a Japanese concentration camp in March 1943. She allowed me free use of all her kitchen things as well as other items. In gratitude I sent her a food package every month at the internment camp. This probably was our best time in Shanghai! With lots of help from your father, I began to bake Viennese-style pastries such as Nussbeugel,

Bischofsbrot, and petit fours.[54] We were kept quite busy. Father delivered the cookies and went shopping. He was happy that things were going so well and that he was well liked by everybody. There also was our "Missie," who put everything at my disposal. She was overjoyed when everything worked well.

Then came the Japanese proclamation, and we had to move to Hongkew.[55] Again, our friends worried about us. We accepted Mr. Schwarz's proposal to convert the large layout hall of a dyeing plant into ten rooms with a single kitchen, and two shower rooms and toilets. Every room was equipped with running water and an electric stove. Obviously, this conversion was expensive. Your father wanted to opt out of this arrangement since we could no longer bake the cookies there, and he didn't want to leave this business. Mr. Schwarz took notice of this and then reported that Mr. Wong, the owner, was interested in your father's business ideas and was willing to hire him. He invited him to try the dyeing business.[56] Mr. Schwarz immediately prepaid one year's rental, and invited your father to start working. He liked your father very much. When some partial payments became due during the construction period, Mr. Schwarz took care of father's share. On August 1, 1943, Mr. Schwarz invited him to his villa in the French quarter. Unfortunately, that was a very hot day for this big event. Since father could not go there by streetcar, he went there partially on foot and partially by rickshaw. He was very tired when he came home. The next day he showed symptoms of a stroke. As I described earlier, he recovered, looked well, but had obviously aged in mind and body. I took care of him from then on. He had much pleasure in his existence. He enjoyed the company of numerous Chinese children in the street. I am very sorry that I could

---

54   *Nussbeugel*: small, nut-filled pastries. *Bischofsbrot*: pound cake filled with nuts and candied fruit. The pastries were sold to Viennese-style coffeehouses that had opened in the International Settlement in Shanghai.

55   On February 18, 1943, the Japanese military commanders in Shanghai, bowing to pressure from the Nazis, issued a proclamation ordering all recently arrived, undocumented refugees to relocate into the Hongkew area within ninety days. There, in the poorest and most crowded district of Shanghai, 18,000–20,000 Jews had to find housing among the hundred thousand Chinese who were already living there. Food was rationed and curfews were imposed.

56   Hans had experience as the owner of the fabric finishing business in Vienna.

not bring him with me, in this state of health. When Mr. Wong heard about your father's illness, he increased his salary to a point where we could almost live on it. But the cost of living kept on increasing; the salary did not. At Christmastime of the same year, father made some dyed blue wool items for Mr. Wong. Father found this a very difficult task. I tried to persuade him to stop doing this. At worst, he would not be paid for his effort. He completed this task. The salary continued until his death, but he could not work anymore. The stories and Mr. Wong's kindness were a daily topic of conversation. A book well worth reading!

Since October 1942 the Engels have been supporting us in a particularly nice manner, without any need for us to remind them. On the contrary, it was Mr. Engel who came to us and asked if we did not already need some money. Through Mrs. Kardos we met Mr. and Mrs. Huber, who were also well disposed toward us by offering some financial support. We never had a need for this money, but your father wanted a financial reserve. I therefore safeguarded this money in case of need. Mr. Schwarz is doing very well personally. He was actually offended that we never accepted money from him.

Actually, he owes some money to a Weiner cousin and would like to pay off some of his debt in this manner. We lacked nothing, as you can see from this. Actually, we were very lucky. Father dreaded the thought of being forced into a retirement home due to lack of money, since that would have been very depressing. Truly, we were always amidst people who brought pleasure to your father. He enjoyed his tarok[57] games with Dr. Sachs, Dr. Freud, and Mr. Weismann until shortly before his last illness. I always served cake and coffee to them, which he enjoyed very much. We always had lots of company. We also have to include Mr. Hans Klinger among our steady visitors. Mr. Klinger has always been very nice and helpful. I can recite a list of perhaps thirty more people who are steady visitors. Usually we served as the social center for these people. The Koll family also lived in our community; just now I am not on the best of terms with them.

---

57   A trick-taking card game played with a tarot deck of seventy-eight cards.

There does not seem to be a specific reason for this tension. We consider them penny-pinching. In spite of our impoverished circumstances we just can't be penny-pinchers. I hope that our debts will not exceed your resources. But we are doing well. Mr. and Mrs. Schwarz are especially nice to us. The Eitelbergs have always provided anything that could cheer up poor father.

Furthermore, a Mr. Fuchs lives near us who used to be a chief nurse in Rekawinkel;[58] he has helped me with father both day and night. He also tried to cheer him up psychologically. Since Mr. Fuchs is alone, I have repaid him by inviting him for supper once a week and he has accepted very happily. There is a Wodicka family who used to live in Floridsdorf[59] who are not too friendly with us. There are also two Duldner families who are very nice. Father really liked Karl Duldner's wife, Luscha, because of her happy outlook, which offered him some distraction from his woes. Some of the others are Mr. Laub, a dental technician, as well as Mr. and Mrs. Eisler. We were—and I am—on very good terms with all of them. We all shared the problems caused by father's period of ill health—and this made our friendships stronger.

Of course, all of them are like my guardians; they all watch that I eat sufficiently and well. But they can't control me—I always do what and how I want to do things. For a while I became a member of the Czech lunch club, where the food was always very good. I had two malaria attacks, which made me give up this eating arrangement.

At the beginning of April, Mr. Engel asked me to take over his household—that took care of me for a while. After all it's no fun to cook for only oneself. Regarding the malaria, I started suffering from it in August 1944. Then father took loving care of me. Naturally, all the ladies among our friends also took care of me. When I had more malaria attacks in March, April, and May, I consulted with Dr. Spaniermann. Now I am undertaking an intensive preventive regime of

---

58   A town in lower Austria
59   A district of Vienna

Atabrine and quinine, with the hope that these attacks will not recur in the future.

Since April 1944 we have been getting financial support from the Joint.[60] I will summarize our debts at the end of this report. Due to this aid we have relieved the Engels of their burden. On the advice of friends I also sold father's possessions to gain additional money and thus not feel in need of funds other than those from the Joint.

I am writing without crying outwardly, but inside I am still moaning. In spite of all the love surrounding me, I can't help remembering father's words during his illness: "You, poor child, will now be alone." While grieving we do remain lonesome. I have decided not to burden my friends with my troubles. Now I keep my resolve. You will probably understand me. I have not been going outside except to shop. However, I get invited by ten different people. Anyone who wants to meet me has to come here. The only exception is a visit to sick people—a *mitzvah*.[61] Right now Mrs. Platschek is very sick. She is a cousin of dear Rudy's cousin Eckstein. I plan to visit her this week since she also came to me.

Yes, I have really lost weight, since the climate wears me down—I don't have to start any weight loss programs.[62] But lately I have been gaining some weight. Now I weigh sixty kilograms; I weighed fifty-six kilograms when your father passed away, so now I have a slender figure. But weight is the least of my worries. I am able and eager to work—that's the only thing that distracts me, helping someone else a little bit.

I have only written about us and myself since that's what you are interested in. If we are not lucky enough to see each other, at least

---

60   The American Jewish Joint Distribution Committee was commonly referred to as the Joint.

61   Hebrew for a good deed

62   J.R.Ross in *Escape to Shanghai* describes living conditions of one family in summer 1943: dinner at the parents' apartment "moldy millet, cracked wheat, half-frozen sweet potatoes …For breakfast they usually ate gruel, a mixture of water, flour and sugar…washed down with green tea; coffee was too expensive…In oppressive summer heat and humidity, it seemed impossible to breathe inside the houses, where mold and mildew grew on food, clothes, linens and shoes…Few people could use fans because electricity was strictly rationed. The ubiquitous insects and mosquitoes added to the discomfort. P. 171–173

you'll hear from me in this way. We have been very happy to receive news from you, even if it consisted of only a few words. Sadly, I cannot write everything that concerns me. But my thoughts are always with you. I am convinced that you have also suffered a lot. These years have not passed unnoticed. There are worries and problems in creating a new life as well as when children are growing up. I sincerely hope that all of you still are in good health, and you are deriving much joy from your children.

There is a very sad chapter when we ask what has happened to all of our dear ones. We sent a letter to Clara in December 1941; it was returned in September 1942 with a notation that the addressee had moved without a new address Father hid this letter, but I found it three months later. You can imagine how we trembled about the fate of all of our loved ones. I have asked you repeatedly if you know anything further, but never received an answer. Obviously, you would have written if you had any favorable information. In early May I tried to write to Clara, Paula, Gabi,[63] and Hirschhaeuter. These letters were accepted. I pray for a reply from any of them. But I don't dare to hope for a response. Somehow I am hoping for a miracle.

Dear Emil, what's new with your parents? What is with Walter[64] and his family? I still want to ask many more questions. I am also very concerned that Rudy writes that the Fred Glaubers will move near his brother.[65] I hope that this is a good sign and that this was caused by a job change. Amen! I cannot visualize the grandchildren. I can remember them only when they left. Meanwhile they have grown and may not have any clear memory of their grandparents. Hitler sent one shot into the bull's-eye, which has torn the families apart. How we have envied you, dear Bertha. Even though you have suffered a

---

63   Gabi was the wife of Erna's brother, Gustav.

64   Emil Glauber's parents and his brother Walter had stayed in Czechoslovakia. They died in Auschwitz. v

65   In 1941 Emil moved to Forest Hills, New York due to a change in his employment. In August 1945, his brother Fred bought the house next door to him. Fred and Susi and their two children, Eve and Steven, lived next door to Emil and Gusti and their two children, Eleanor and George, for the rest of their lives. Gusti, the last of the four, died in 2007.

great deal, at least you have been lucky enough to see your children and grandchildren. May God grant you many more years to enjoy this good fortune. It is difficult to contemplate the sad fate that we were just ready to leave, but did not have the same luck. But it makes no sense to speculate. I have also been saying that being alone is a terrible fate. But you also cannot keep thinking with hindsight. Just like cattle! We sleep and drink while the years keep passing along. We may vegetate, but we have to thank God when we remain healthy. Hongkew is not an ideal place to live. What I mostly regret is that there is not a spot, no little bench, where father could have enjoyed himself. Only in front of our house there is a spot that resembles Kagran. That place made me feel sort of at home—your father could sit down and spend the evening out there if he could not remain in the apartment any longer. This year I don't want to go downstairs anymore—it is dark and perhaps a bit spooky outside.

Continued on 7 August 1945

I took a long break in writing this report. Perhaps I was not always in the mood. I am still with the Engel family since Mrs. Engel isn't well yet. She always has an elevated temperature. She really needs much better surroundings, which we cannot find around here.

This year's summer is very heavy. The heat is also getting to me. But we can survive the circumstances if there is peace again. On July 17, 1945,[66] there was a terrible catastrophe here when an air raid killed not only many hundreds of Chinese, but also about fifty refugees. Many others suffered serious injuries and are still being treated. During the raid I was at the Engels, so I was not personally affected. A bomb impacted about three minutes from us. Our fellow apartment dwellers just had to suffer through the scare. We are also very much in danger since we live in the middle of a factory area. Our

---

66   The allies flying under heavily overcast skies bombed Hongkew. They were heading for the Chiangwan Airdrome north of Shanghai. Some bombs had been dropped too early. Two hundred and fifty people including thirty-one refugees were killed, five hundred were wounded, and seven hundred were left homeless.

men have built a shelter, which will offer protection to a few people. I would be safer there. I probably could have gotten official permission to move due to my advanced age. However, there is only a minimal chance of getting a room there, and at great expense. As God wills it!

There is also terrible inflation, which makes living here insanely expensive. This does not affect me too much since I am eating at the Engels. We are lucky that the Joint still operates here. They have been unbelievably effective. Even though there are always complainers, we have to recognize that it is not easy for JDC to help the people here. We are all tired of just vegetating here, without any real future, nor with real hope of survival. One of us, your dear father, has already fallen by the wayside.

23 August 1945   Shanghai

From Erna

Dearest children and grandchildren,

It is finally possible to write you directly instead of via our former landlady. It hurts me very much that I have to write you the terribly sad news about the passing of your dear father. I don't know if the letters sent via the Red Cross have reached you with the same sad news. Exactly six months ago to the day, the poor man closed his eyes after a very serious illness that lasted ten weeks. Sad to say, his last wish, "I'd like to see my children again," was not fulfilled.

He was a very popular person to everyone he knew and liked everyone he could meet. All I talk about is us; and you know that all my thoughts are about you, my dearest children. I am extremely interested in all the goings-on of you and your children. I just cannot imagine what they look like when they are so much grown up, compared to how they looked when you left.

There is a very sad thought that preoccupies my mind both day and night: what has happened to all our dear ones whom I left behind? But regrettably I imagine that they have met with very little good. Otherwise, they would have responded to my various letters. But please do tell me of any news about them, no matter how bad the truth may be. Right now, I don't want to rage about those Nazi criminals who are responsible for all that evil. I really hope that they will be punished in due time, but our dead will not come back to life. Hopefully, all you my very dearest are in good health and satisfied with your careers. I read in one of the letters from you, my dear Weiners, that my dear Glaubers, are about to move into your brother's neighborhood. Therefore I just don't know where you are now. In any case, I hope that you are all healthy. You all must have worked very hard, and I can imagine that life in America is not that easy.

Now to talk about myself. I am in good health; and for the past five months I have been the housekeeper at the Engels. Mrs. Engel developed some lung problems at the beginning of April. Even though there is an eighteen-year-old daughter, she is still attending school. I eat lunch with them every day—this provides a purpose for my life. I really enjoy hearing from Mrs. Engel that she always calms down when she spots my gray-haired head at her door. Just before the end of the war Mrs. Engel said that she is going to get loud reproaches from her children about abusing me. But I would be very happy to receive such a letter of reproach! And of course we got the news of the war's end after some very difficult nights—the 17 July bombardment of our Hongkew area led to many casualties among our fellow emigrants. After all, living through a war is a terrible experience. What are all of our dear ones doing, such as the Blochs, Mawei, the Maglaus, all the dear nieces and nephews, Elli and Fredi and the others whose names I cannot cite here—please send my warmest greetings to all of them.

I want to remind you that all my papers identify me as Ernestine; presumably, I will have to use a Czech quota number.[67] My birth date is 12 March 1884. I plan to try very hard to leave on an evacuation ship; I hope that the people here will help me do so. At this time we owe money only to the Engels and to the Joint. We also had borrowed some money from the Hubers, but we returned it to them just before the first bombardment, when we didn't really need that money. I can only repeat again that all the people here have been exceptionally nice to me. These loans spared me the need to enter a retirement facility, as well as the need to borrow more money. So please don't send any more money; if I need any more, I will let you know.

Lot of kisses and hugs to you all, my dearest ones, and much love from your Mother

---

67   Immigration quotas were based on the number of United States residents from all countries in the census of 1920. Since Erna was born in Czechoslovakia she was in the Czechoslovakian quota, which had more spaces than the Austrian quota.

27 August 1945   Shanghai

from Erna

My dear children and grandchildren, as well as all other dear ones,

Last week I already wrote you through Mrs. Boeckbinder. Now I have heard that emigrants here can send mail directly via the Clipper planes; therefore I am also using this opportunity again, but I don't know which letter will reach you. After many years of just hoping, a family get-together is now foreseeable. I am assuming that you have already received some news about me where I wrote about the sad passing of your dear father. You can imagine the pain in my heart that that poor man did not survive until he could see his dearly beloved children and grandchildren.

We surely want to think of him in love, in what we have lost with him, and you know that as well as I. He just was not an ordinary human being, and was loved by everyone in his surroundings. Fritz Duldner just told me that this letter needs to be ready within five minutes to reach the plane.

So now I am rushing to move all levers that can help me search for any and all possibilities for emigrating from here. You can rest assured that I am doing everything possible, and the other people here are also trying to help me. If you can intervene in the USA, please remember that all my papers use the name Ernestine Mayer; my birth date is 12 March 1884. My next letter will include more details.

May all of you feel kissed frequently and lovingly by your loving Mother

This undated, handwritten note was included with Erna's letter of 27 August, which Karl Duldner delivered directly to the airport. The name of the addressee is illegible.

Dear Mr.

Right now, we are in an awful hurry since we are at the airport. Our family has been living all by ourselves in an industrial plant. We are really happy that everything is now over. We have had enough of the bombardment; we have been living under very dangerous conditions. In front of our house there is a black area. Nearby there is a large bomb crater surrounded by destroyed industrial plants. Thanks be to God, every other building seems to be intact. Now we have enough food to eat, just as in the dear peacetime, but it is very expensive. One gold dollar is now worth two hundred thousand Shanghai dollars. Now the value of the Shanghai dollar has dropped even further. We are thinking of all of you. Let's get away from here! The climate is just terrible.

Warmest greetings to you all, Karl Duldner

5 September 1945 Shanghai

From Erna

My dearest ones

Now this is my third letter that I have written without a single sign of life from you. So I have to be patient since none of the other refugees here have received any mail either. You probably already have received the sad news that your poor father was unfortunate not to live long enough to meet you again. And I cannot tell you enough how much that thought has been depressing me, that this poor man couldn't live long enough for that to happen. But to our common regret we need to content ourselves with that fact. It should be comforting for you to know that he lacked for nothing, and was surrounded by helpful and empathetic people. These same people continue to treat me in the same manner, and also act as my important personal advisors when possible. But since you know me so well, I try to minimize my reliance on them. Now it is almost four weeks since peace has returned, and we were completely surprised by that event. We could have never believed in such a quick end. Apparently the atomic bomb seems to have been the deciding element. But I don't want to talk politics; I am just very happy that the war has ended. I hope to be lucky enough to hug my dear ones very soon. That is the only thing in this entire world that still holds my interest. I don't want to ask too many questions, but hope that you will write to me in great detail very soon about yourselves, your children, and all the other loved ones.

I am also very lonesome for all the people that I left behind in the homeland. I still wonder what these poor people have suffered. I am just afraid that the worst may have happened to them. But please write the truth to me. I have written registered mail to Miss Hohenberg, to Gabi in Pilsen, and to Paula in Prague, but have received no sign of life from any of them. So now I am very afraid to receive any news about them. For example, about your parents, dear Emil, and Walter and his entire family. It is absolutely terrible what crimes those Nazi criminals have committed.

And we continue to exist. There are so many times when I just can't help thinking about all of them. In general, we have spent our years here doing relatively well, and need to thank the good Lord that we were privileged to do so. Yesterday Mrs. Boeckbinder, our previous landlady, visited me; she has always been very nice to me. Father liked her very much. She told me that she had to move into the Hongkew camp, so she offered me her bed. We swapped a bed for her couch, but it is not comfortable to sleep on. But the couch should not be blamed for that; my health bears more of that responsibility. I have had to take time off for the past week since I have several infected fingers that Dr. Egon—lovingly—and I have to take care of.

Now this sheet of paper is completely filled, and so I have to end this letter. I hope that all of you are healthy and satisfied in your jobs.

All my love to the grandchildren. Many kisses and hugs, your Mother and Grandmother

20 September 1945   Shanghai

From Erna

All of my dearest ones,

I would like to keep the promise to myself to write on a weekly basis. So now here is my letter. Regrettably, I still have not received the letter that I have been aching for. A lot of mail from the United States was expected around Yom Kippur, but there was nothing for me. You probably had some very sad High Holidays since they are the first ones after your dear father's passing.

My thoughts have focused on him and on you. As you might guess, I have been thinking of the High Holidays one year ago. I am really sick at the thought that he did not live long enough to see peace again. He would have really enjoyed peacetime since he was so interested in everything. But sad to say, you have to be satisfied with your own life. We hope that you prayed for the very best for yourselves, and that your fast went well. I was also in Temple, a movie theater. May the Almighty hear all of our desires! Up to now He has always protected us and kept us from harm; we should never underestimate the fact that miraculously we have been saved. The situation here was worse than critical; the bombardment of Shanghai surely would have continued. Now we are living here in a jubilant state. Sailors and soldiers are greeted enthusiastically. After four years of living in a dead city, now there is a lot going on. The day before yesterday I visited dear father's grave. Then the Bleiers got a hold of me and I could admire the loud goings-on from an electric streetcar. The Japanese have to leave Shanghai by tomorrow morning; now they have been limited to a "designated area." Actually, the Japanese were never as bad as the Nazis; but neither did the Japanese display any nice feelings for us. But now that episode has ended. Now we are counting the days until, God willing, we can be together again. Right now, there is no local American consulate in operation, and presumably we will need new affidavits.

If I hear anything I will start dealing with the emigration situation. And I am convinced that if you can do something more in the United States, then you will take the proper action. But I guess that now we are getting quite impatient. Everything here is proceeding at a snail's pace, but I can also foresee that Shanghai faces some overwhelming tasks, particularly since the end came so fast for the Allied Powers. Now we can write to people all over the world. Therefore tomorrow I plan to write to Prague, Pilsen, and Vienna. I am tortured by the fact that I haven't heard from any of these people; perhaps by some sort of miracle some of them may still be alive, even though the newspapers have reported that there is no hope. That seems to be a terribly sad situation that leaves us in total disbelief.

Otherwise I am in good health, my fingers seem to work properly again, and as of Monday I start to spend time with the Engels. They are very attached to me; I am delighted to make better use of my time. I have been a lazy bones long enough! I need to stay in shape for when I come to you. I don't want to get into the habit of being lazy.

Since I now have lots of spare time, I started to reread all your "recent" letters. After four years, all the letters I have from you are dated during 1941! So now the world has acquired an entirely new face. In my mind, I am in your midst—that offers me a wonderful personal distraction. How are the children doing? They have grown up and thus may cause you new problems. What are they studying? In my mind I am convinced they have developed their desires and know what they plan to choose as a career. You, my dear Glaubers, now have a very grown-up daughter; most likely Lore already dreams of going to dances and other fun things suitable for her age. It's nice to know that you are living in such a beautiful country. Sad to say, here the young people cannot do much, since we have been restricted to Hongkew district. Here there are no trees or parks. Instead sometimes they go to bars; obviously that's not to everybody's taste. I can observe that with Eva Engel; she is a very nice young lady, but is subject to very many constraints. She sometimes gets together with the younger daughter of the architect, Mr. Fischer; the young lady usually is off in her cloud. Mrs. Fischer never seems to cross my path, so we normally don't meet. Initially Mr. Fischer was very busy with his move to Hongkew, but that activity has stopped by now. Right now he has been hospitalized for observation. I believe that Mrs. Fischer is maintaining their home and seems very overworked. Apparently their older daughter is engaged. Whom else are you interested in? The Kollmanns are doing reasonably well. Liesel doesn't look well and receives periodic liver shots, as most people seem to need here.

Everybody here is trying to lose weight, especially the women. But I am particularly proud of Mrs. Engel, for whom I am caregiver; she has actually gained fourteen kilograms. But I am not really responsible for that gain: she went through a diabetic medical routine that included bed rest. Now I am fairly slender and weigh about sixty kilograms and really feel very well at that weight. Our summer here has been very tough: it was very hot for three months, without any rain. But by now we have survived the worst of it and I hope to spend the next summer with you. We hope to hold out until then. After all, since the start of the Hitler era we have been subjected to eternal waiting periods. Regrettably, your poor father didn't make it—some people just cannot wait forever. I want nothing more than to get lots of detailed news from my dear ones about all of you, including your children. What are all the Blochs doing, the Rosensteins, Neubauers, Ellises, Paul Schratter, as well as all the nephews and nieces? I am really very interested in everybody and everything.

My neighbors are very nice and kind—the twenty people get along very well, except for some petty incidents. The Karl Duldner family already has visas for Sweden, but cannot travel there directly; they told me that they would travel with me via America. I am very satisfied with that proposed travel arrangement and would love to wave goodbye as soon as possible. So that's enough for today! Want to kiss each of you often and a lot.

Longing for you

Your Mother and Grandmother

Mr. Witt is taking this letter with him to America to forward it from there. Today I am very sad because Mrs. Kardos passed away after a long illness. Poor lady! Just now when she could have hugged her beloved son so very soon. She was a very good friend and a neighbor on Bubbling Well Road; and now she will be dear father's neighbor in the cemetery, close to Kreise's mother.

28 September 1945   Shanghai

All my dearest ones,

The Goodwill Commission did not accept the attached letters for forwarding, so Mrs. Boeckbinder is kind enough to take this letter with her when she visits next Sunday; that's the way I am trying to satisfy my obligation to schmooze with you on a weekly basis. My hands are doing fairly well by now, so I have started to work again at the Engels—everybody is very happy with this arrangement. In fact, I am very proud of the fact that the people around here find me so popular; in fact, I have received two separate job offers as a housekeeper! What do you say to that?

I usually tell these people that you can't make me do that for money; I'll only do that for love and for being treated very nicely. So therefore I am overjoyed that I can earn a living at age sixty-one. But I would really love to be your housekeeper. So you should save your torn stockings and laundry until my arrival.

Actually, due to the presence of so many military people here there has been an upswing for the local coffeehouses and bars.

A very sad event occurred that made me go out last Sunday and Monday; there was a big to-do; I believe that it could not have been any livelier in America. I have already written you that Mrs. Kardos has died after a very short and severe illness. In the past I would visit her occasionally when I visited dear Father's grave site; on those occasions I found her looking sickly, but that type of unhealthy appearance is quite common here—and usually we tend to blame the heat. I just didn't know that she had been sick; I would have been happy to do some favor for her. I also heard that she had asked for me. That's just a very sad story. She had survived the war quite well, had earned a lot of money, and yearned to be again reunited with her only son; but that's all water over the dam. And she was only fifty years old. She was particularly nice to us, and helped us find our apartment in her apartment building; Father felt particularly comfortable in that apartment. So now she has been cremated, and thus became father's neighbor. It is exactly seven months since his passing. But life just keeps going on.

To my regret I still have had no news from you, and my longing to hear everything about you is just increasing steadily. Some U.S. mail has started to arrive here, but to my regret I was not one of the lucky ones. I am absolutely certain that this cannot be your fault. So I have comforted myself by rereading your old letters. Now these letters are four years old; a lot must have happened in the meantime. And now we also are finding out exactly what happened in the concentration camps; we follow these news reports with much fear all day and night long. I am still hoping for a miracle, but we cannot get any additional news. Currently people can watch newsreel reports about the camp at Auschwitz, but I cannot get up the nerve to view them myself. It was an absolute miracle that Otto Fischer could recognize his brother from Prague; the film showed him in very bad physical shape, but alive! The day before yesterday I met Mrs. Platschek, his sister-in-law. Right now she is very ill with sprue, a tropical disease, and she just seems to be wasting away. I am going to write in English to my grandchildren so that they can make fun of their old grandmother. I have absolutely no opportunity to speak English, but I am reading English books.

Please feel kissed and really hugged
Your Mother

8 October 1945   Shanghai

From Erna

All my dearest ones,

I just cannot tell you how excited I was with sheer pleasure when Dr. Perl handed me a letter dated 13 September.[68] I have been waiting for a sign of life from you, but nothing ever came. I went shopping with Luscha Duldner earlier this morning and she got the newspaper from the carrier, then the first thing I did was to check for any mail. So I said to her, "I'm sure that I won't get any mail," but then I spotted it! This was still well before nine. And of course I was completely convinced in my own mind that this letter was from my sister—you just cannot imagine how happy I felt! I just couldn't concentrate on anything; I was absolutely speechless to find out that you, my dear Weiners, now are in California! So now I am extremely curious about the reason for your relocation! The Weiners had already told me in a Red Cross letter that you, my dear Glaubers, had moved again.[69] I am very sorry that you now reside so far apart. That just means that I'll be unable to enjoy both families in one place. But let neither of you be unhappy. And now we do need to thank the good Lord that all of you have survived the war well and in good health. To our regret we have suffered the very major loss. By now you know that your dear father was not lucky enough to live long enough for our reunion. He would have really enjoyed that. And that would have been so very nice! He truly ached for his children and grandchildren! In fact, he had lost all interest in the war situation. How frequently he said, "I want to go to my children!" Thinking of that phrase still hurts to this very day.

---

68   This letter may have been from someone else relating the news of her family. See the 12 November letter when she has received the "first letter with all the details."

69   In June 1945 Kärhe and Rudy Weiner and their children moved to Oakland, California, where the climate was better for Rudy's asthma. The Glaubers had moved from Cleveland to New York in 1941.

There's a lot more to tell, but I don't want to get into all the details here. On the whole, you can say that we never lacked for anything. Thanks be to God, we have run into many people here whom we had met earlier and who had already been holding us in high esteem. For example, Engel has offered good advice and other significant support all along. He did lend us some money when needed; we have spent these funds frugally and with much forethought. Later on I will detail our local debts. In addition, sometimes we have used funds provided by the Joint; their staff has been exceptionally nice to us. Please don't send us any money for the time being! Right now I am spending at least ten dollars per month. As I have written you previously, I have served as the Engels' housekeeper for more than six months since Mrs. Engel developed her lung problem. There is an amah there to do all the major housework. Normally I do the shopping and cooking, and take care of Mrs. Engel's personal needs; generally I leave the Engels around three. I have been very happy to help out there; that has satisfied my personal desire to remain a useful human being. But I am just sorry for the reason. Actually, I could have had several such jobs because there is such a demand for my services. Since I eat my lunch at the Engels, my other expenses have been lowered, in spite of the fact that life is extremely expensive here and that the dollar value has shrunk so much. And I still have some stuff in reserve—your father was always in favor of having things in reserve. In fact, occasionally I sell some of my reserve canned goods and soap! I am writing you this only to confirm the fact that I am doing quite well over here. And I cannot complain about anything else; several other people keep a close eye on me, and are available to me for many types of advice and support.

Now I have written enough about myself, so it's your turn: I'd like to know if you are satisfied with your lives, and how the grandchildren are doing with their studies. Can they still remember their grandparents? I do have many questions for you, and hope to receive very detailed reports from you very soon. And right now I am still very pained by the thought of what has happened to all our beloved relatives and friends whom we have left behind in that hell, Paula,

Clara, Gaby, Emma, dear Emil's parents, and the many Bergers. I am interested in knowing about them, but I am shaking with fear for all of them. It is just too terrible to read about the tragic happenings. But all of us are hoping for some miracles! There are just no words to describe those murderers. Let's hope that there will be some retribution for their evil deeds, but that will never revive the many dead people!

So now I want to stop this letter; I'd rather write more frequently. So please stay well, feel often and lovingly kissed—including the Blochs, Neubauers, and all the others of importance to us! With the greatest love and eagerly looking forward to letters.

Your Mother and Grandmother

19 October 1945 Shanghai

From Erna

All my dearest ones,

I don't want to let this week pass by without schmoozing a little
bit with you, my dearest ones. I am still chewing on the news that
Dr. Perl brought to me. As a result my disposition seems to be a lot
sunnier now. I am still trying to figure out why you, my dear Weiners, chose to move to California, and what you are going to be doing
there. But I am quite certain that you have done the right thing. And
when I am lucky enough to see you again, it will be easier to meet
you. I hope that you will be living near where I will be landing. But
you, my dear Glaubers, will be somewhat farther away. But when I
arrive, I hope for an early opportunity to visit you too. According to a
local rumor, the consulate is to start operating again as of next week.
Apparently, some people will have it easier if they already had a visa
previously. But to my regret that probably will not apply to me. We
had already been to the consulate, had completed the medical examinations, and were supposed to return on 11 December 1941. But I
still don't have the visa. Because of the elapsed time I will probably
need a new affidavit, but you know more about that over there than
I do here. You can imagine how depressed I am because your father
could not live long enough for this chance. This thought always still
bothers me, but with God's regrets I need to keep facing this fact,
even though it is so hard to bear that memory.

Today's letter is mainly intended for my dear children with birthdays around now. First of all are you, dear Käthe, whose birthday
was just a short time ago—I wish you all the best, love, nice things,
and only joy. You all have been through enough by now. There will
be a lot to tell when we will meet again. Now I want to congratulate you for the birthdays of dear Emil and dear Rudy. I just figured out that you, dear Rudy, are not yet forty. Please excuse my
attempt to make you feel much older at this time. Nevertheless I

want you to feel my many hearty birthday kisses. Please know that you are very appreciated—may you have all the good things that a loving mother's heart could wish for you. You now have many years of hard work behind you and probably also ahead of you. May the good Lord keep you healthy for many years, while surrounded by your loving family. And I pray for the chance to share some of these times directly with you. Then I can verify with my own eyes that all of you are doing well. That wish is the core of my life's desires, and I truly want nothing more than that. But that wish is really not very modest.

Everybody here is predicting that I will be leaving very soon, but I won't believe that until I can wave good-bye from aboard the ship. I have also been told that I may be able to acquire Czech citizenship again. I am not making such promises to myself, but I will try to do that. Perhaps then somebody can do something about our property in Pilsen. Right now I am doing fairly well. I stay at the Engels every day until three o'clock. I do their housework and am very happy to be busy in that way. I also hope to keep quite busy in your home. That is the only activity that satisfies me and allows me to spend my time productively. Please don't send me any money. I will let you know when I need more money. I have been receiving living expenses from the Joint here. When it will get down to the travel expense, I will have no problem in borrowing it from Mr. Schwarz, or Huber, or Engel. You can rest assured that all of our friends are truly caring and very attentive to our needs. Therefore your father never lacked for anything. I continue to be extremely depressed about what has happened to all of our dear relatives and friends. So please don't leave out any answers about them; any specific knowledge about their fate would seem better since the uncertainty is keeping me awake at night. Over here we hear only about a few miracles that some individuals did survive; but to our regret the majority of the news is all entirely tragic. And I ache for every one of them. Obviously, I am much more interested in all of your lives and activities. So I don't want to ask too many questions about the others, but I am still very curious about their fates.

How is Lore doing? Of course she will have to make her career choice, what she wants to study, and what her talents are. Regrettably the times are such that one needs to think of practical goals. The boys still have time.[70] Lieserl, the little flea, was only two when I saw her for the last time; now she probably is a grown-up student. Actually I wanted to communicate with the children in English, but I am afraid that they will only laugh at me, and therefore lose all respect for me. I just have to say *nebbich*.[71]

The Engels have a lively seven-year-old grandson who may resemble Schurli; that is, both are "all boy" kids. The children here have been living a fairly poor life, but their lot has been improving since the end of the war; they can now visit the only park in this part of Hongkew. Last week was the first time I went to that park with Mrs. Engel; now I have promised myself that I will go there more frequently. Here we have totally forgotten what a tree or a grassy area looks like. I was always very sorry for your father that he could walk only along the very dirty streets; he was just delighted when he had to do an errand. How are the dear Blochs doing? Most likely they must have been very deeply touched by your father's death. I hope that they are well and that Felix and his family are also doing well. Also, how are the Rosensteins, the Neubauers, the Ellises, and Paul Schratter?

So enough schmoozing for today. All my dear ones, please be and stay well, and feel kissed by your
Mother
Grandmother

---

70   In 1945, Lore {Eleanor} was sixteen. The "boys" (Henry and George) were twelve, and Lieserl was nine years old.
71   That's too bad

30 October 1945 Shanghai

All of my beloved ones,

After writing my dear Glaubers, yesterday, your dear telegram arrived today for which I'd like to thank you. It's just such a wonderful
feeling that you think of me so much. It is so sad to say—and I have
to repeat myself—that your dear father didn't survive long enough
because he yearned so much for his children and grandchildren. He
longed "to be with his children" just so very shortly before the war's
end, but to everyone's regret he just didn't make it. I have already
written so many letters to tell you everything but I just don't know
which of them you have received. When I found out from Dr. Perl
that you had moved, that news came like a bolt of lightning from the
sky! I hope that all of you are healthy and that you, dear Rudy, are
happy with your job. I assume that now you are back in your former
type of business. Or was that move due to the fact that you could
not take Chicago's climate? Obviously, I'd like to know as much as
possible about you so please tell me everything in very much detail!
Yesterday I wrote to the dear Glaubers, but had to leave one sheet
behind because I didn't have enough money with me for the postage.
In that letter I did ask for some pictures; so now I want to repeat that
request. From the looks of things here it will still be much more time
until I can join you; so therefore I'd like to enjoy your pictures in the
meantime. That's at least as much that's worth telling, or in this case
writing. After all, the letters sent via the Red Cross represent just
a "sign of life!" I just hope that you and your children are healthy,
as well as Mawei, the Blochs, and all my other loved ones. I am extremely worried about all the people left behind in the old country.
Please tell me whatever you know. I am fully aware of the possibility
that to everybody's regret one cannot expect any good news; it's just
true that in our subconscious there is a hope for some sort of miracle.
Here and there we hear a little bit of positive news, but most of the
time the news is very sad. This year our summer was exceptionally
oppressive. The time of extreme heat, bombs, and always a lack of
lights are now behind us; actually we don't lack for anything here.

I have spent the entire summer with the Engels. Mrs. Engel is suffering from a lung ailment. Thank God, she is doing better now; she is allowed to go for walks outside. Today she visited me for coffee; we celebrated the arrival of your dear telegram. But so far her doctor has not allowed her to go back to work. At the Engels I am being treated like a family member; I am also very happy that I can be of some service to them. Only that very occupation has enabled me to survive the most difficult time of my life! If I can contribute even the smallest bit of good to the world, that fact makes me feel much better. My neighbors were absolutely wonderful to me during your father's illness. They were at my disposal both day and night, so I didn't have to take him to a hospital. You can rest assured that he didn't lack for anything, and that he literally died in my arms. We had never discussed what to do with his mortal remains, but I had his body cremated so I would not have to leave him here all by himself. I always told him, whenever he was desperately depressed, "We will travel to America together!" Thus I would like to keep my promise to him even though we had planned to do that in an entirely different manner. But all my complaints went for naught! Even though that sounds so sad, we just need to be satisfied with our lot. I still miss him all the time and everywhere; I can just imagine how this loss has affected you. Please continue thinking of your father with love!

Mr. Engel is planning to hand this letter to a lady who is about to leave for America tomorrow; therefore this letter should reach you very soon! I have already written another letter that is supposed to travel with the first repatriation ship, as well as one to be sent with the Goodwill Mission; but all these letters were sent to the Chicago address—so I don't know if they will reach you. I just got this letter back because the lady actually was not leaving immediately. Therefore I am omitting the third sheet because the extra postage is so expensive. I'd rather write another letter next week. The cost would jump from 150 to 270 new Chinese dollars using the new currency. It's very hard to figure out the value of the new currency!

As I have already told you repeatedly, here in Hongkew we are now living in a factory, formerly a bleachery. We are twenty people. They have converted a large factory room into rooms. There are nine women who cook in a kitchen; usually the goings-on are peaceful there. But some arguments do occur because twenty people are not always of the same opinions! We have two commodes, two showers—considered very ample for Hongkew. Each of us could move somewhere else, but any such move must be literally paid for in gold by weight! Supposedly, we can stay here for another six months, but perhaps—God willing—I'll be on my way to you by then.

I still want to go to the consulate later this week. I can register there, but then I need to wait until new papers have arrived. I am assuming that you will keep checking on my progress over there; up to now nobody here has been able to accomplish anything. So I just have to continue to have patience. To my regret, nothing is happening here as I had imagined earlier. The inflation here is terrible: consumer prices are rising by the hour, but the dollar is not keeping up! Now a one-pound loaf of bread costs eighteen thousand dollars; one egg is five to six thousand dollars; sugar is one hundred forty to two thousand dollars; one pound of coffee is one million dollars. Pretty terrible!! But don't worry about me! First, I have lunch at the Engels; second, I still have some extra food at home. All of that lets me muddle through! In essence, this is now a very strange place—you can buy anything you want; the only problem is the cost!

I am delighted to hear that your—dear Rudy's—sisters are doing so well. And I am very impressed by Mawei, who has become so self-reliant. Based on that fact I now think that there will be a chance for me to join you!

During the time before we had to move to Hongkew I used to make Nussbeugel and Bischofsbrot, as well as some other Viennese baked delicacies, on an "assembly line" basis. Your father was my manager; that period was our most pleasant time here. At that time we lived on Bubbling Well Road with a Dutch landlady, Mrs. Boeckbinder. She treated us extremely well; now she still eats with me every Sunday. She used to place her entire kitchen and all her utensils at my disposal so that I didn't have to buy any extra kitchen gadgets. But I plan to tell you all about that when we get together.

I visited the consulate again without any success; they are still not working on any visa matters. And I cannot proceed on anything without an affidavit. Now I want to repeat my personal data, just to be sure: Ernestine Mayer, 12 March 1884. What would happen if somebody finds a hair in the soup by spotting the first name Erna! There is a local rumor that all Jewish emigrants have to leave by March. But so many other rumors are circulating here, that particular rumor may prove untrue.

Previously I wrote to Gusti that the Engels may need their money very soon, and to have it ready for payment. The amount is $850[72] plus interest; I cannot judge if this amount needs to be revaluated. The interest amount should be on the interest rate paid by the New York savings bank. In any case I think that an extra $100 will take care of the revaluation.

I hope that this particular transaction will not strain your finances. If necessary, you can sell my jewelry. I also owe the Joint 573 Swiss francs, but there is no immediate rush to repay this debt. I don't want to take any more advantage of that particular source of funds. I have sold your dear father's things, so now I have a total savings of $340. I wholeheartedly believe that I can use some of that money for my ship's ticket since I currently spend at most $10 per month for myself. It seems evident that you should take whichever of your dear father's possessions that you will be able to use. I have a new suit with light stripes: can you use it or should I sell it? In addition there is father's fur sports jacket. Anything can be sold here! I am certain that I can get $10 gold for the suit. If father didn't have such short arms I could have sold it for at least $15. I sold some bedclothes since I had more than enough. I still have a good double bed, but I am waiting to hear if you can use it.

Based on my experiences I have become very superstitious: I won't sell anything until I have the affidavit in my hands. Nothing can be done before then at the consulate; in the meantime they only seem to deal with people whom they have called already.

Feel kissed lovingly and frequently—
Your Mother

---

72    $850 would be about $8,700 in 2006

The following undated letter to Emil appears to be from Mr. Schwarz. He was living outside the ghetto in the French concession. He and the Engels had been very helpful to Erna and Hans ever since their arrival in Shanghai. Gusti Glauber's replies to him and to her mother are dated 9 January 1946. Mr. Schwarz's concerns seem contradictory to Erna's repeated remarks about her pleasure in helping the Engels and taking meals with them, which helped her financial situation.

My dear Mr. Glauber,

Here are a few words that should bypass Mrs. Mayer's censorship. She was most insistent on reading what I am trying to write to you. Please don't think badly of me, but I need to say what is close to my heart. Mr. Engel doesn't seem to be a very nice person, since he is apparently really abusing Mrs. Mayer's good nature. This is not only my private opinion, but it seems to be shared by everyone else who knows the situation here. It is a fact that Mrs. Engel got sick and dear Mrs. Mayer was searching for something to do during her spare time.

It is absolutely unnecessary for Mrs. Mayer to act as a caregiver for Mrs. Engel. Thanks be to God, Mr. Engel does have the financial means to hire a household servant. Furthermore, the Engels' daughter lives in that household, is young and healthy, and seems to be well taken care of. During the current cold weather Mrs. Mayer should not be expected to run attendance on the Engels; she shouldn't serve as a cook in their cold kitchen, especially under miserable sanitary conditions— all that work for just a little bit of food. You, dear Mr. Glauber, are under no obligation to allow this sad situation to continue. Mr. Engel seems to act like a good guy, but actually he seems to be a very calculating guy. Apparently he has arranged for a very favorable transfer of funds to a secure location, and wants to be admired for this as a heavenly angel. And then he has twisted things around so much that he has made you feel obligated to him. As of now Mrs. Mayer has done more than enough; therefore, I would like to ask Mrs. Mayer to request that Mrs. Engel give her leave so that she can rest up for a while. She would love to sleep longer in the morning, and not leave her home in all kinds of weather since everybody has become accustomed to having all the food delivered, instead of the lady of the house going shopping.

Please don't ever mention this letter, but I feel duty-bound to tell you about this situation.

Please don't consider this letter as an expression of hate toward Mr. Engel. I really get along with him quite well even though he seems to be a know-it-all. I sincerely believe in the governing principle that I try very hard to get along with every other human being, and I still believe that this principle also applies to the Engels. But I would like to see Mrs. Mayer get her well-deserved peace and quiet. I have the impression that she no longer wants to take care of Mrs. Engel, but that she doesn't have the nerve to stop because of her overwhelming feeling of gratitude. So please send an urgent request to your dear mother, from America, to preserve her strength and stay home in her warm house so that she may continue to live a wonderful life. Enough lady visitors come to the house to provide lots of distraction; she will also have the time to write letters, instead of staying up very late to write. So now you know what's really bothering me.

Sincerely yours,
Schwarz

12 November 1945 Shanghai

From Erna

All my dearest ones,

I cannot tell you how overjoyed I was on Saturday when the first letter with all the details from you reached my hands. I really longed for the first sign of life from you, and finally it arrived! I hope that it will be followed by many more detailed letters. After these many years have elapsed one has to ask for a lot of information about everything. Many thanks for your kind words of sympathy about father's passing. None of us can forget him. I cry for him and don't complain. But I have promised myself not to become a burden to my neighbors, and I am trying to keep that promise. I still miss him always and everywhere. But nobody can change the sad fact. First of all, I would like to congratulate all my dear children with November birthdays; normally I have done that ahead of time, but I still want to send you lots of luck, the best of health, and lots of success in your careers. After all, it's your fortieth, dear Rudy, and dear Emil's fiftieth; these are special birthdays that should not pass unnoticed. It would have been so nice to deliver my wishes in person, but that will have to be postponed until we are together again. But I am with you in spirit, and I am delivering my usual birthday kisses. Then it will be dear Schurli's birthday; now I just hope to at least attend the dear boy's Bar Mitzvah after joining you.

Last week I received another three Red Cross letters from the Glaubers dated October 1944, May 25, and July 20. So the mail is reaching me only by the tablespoon. Thanks be to God, the bad times are now over. Your dear letter doesn't drop a hint to me as to what has happened to our loved ones. The worries about them hound me day and night. I do know there isn't much hope for any of them, but all of us are hoping for some sort of miracle. In any case, please do write me about whatever you may have found out about them. As soon as war ended in Germany, I immediately wrote to the Hirsch family in

Vienna, as well as to Prague and Pilsen; but obviously I got no reply from any of them. No mail for Europe has been accepted here for many weeks already. So now I got your letter, dear Käthe. First of all, I want to congratulate you on getting a little house; may you spend only good days there! So now I am really curious why you moved away from Chicago. Did you, dear Rudy, lose your job there, or did you resign from it? Or were you unable to take Chicago's climate? I am of the opinion that your hay fever has always created problems for you. Or did you find a much better job? And dear Käthe, are you still struggling by doing massages? You probably also have many household chores, even when the children are so sweet. I would love to take over your household chores. I am most eager to work; only that type of work has helped me to survive my difficult times. I have written repeatedly to expedite my emigration. But such speeded-up emigration matters occur only rarely. So now let me end this letter. I plan to send an airmail letter every Monday. The next time I will write to dear Emil.

Stay well, all my love. Please kiss the dear children.

Be hugged and kissed
your Mother

The following letter was from Gerhard Karplus. He was the husband of Gertrude "Gerti" Malz. Gerti's stepsister Ellie was married to Franz Mayer, a brother of Hans. As a soldier in the United States Army, stationed in Shanghai, Gerhard was able to help Erna with her correspondence and in other ways.

<u>In English</u>
G. E. Karplus—
1st Lt. Corps of Engineers
Shanghai Base COMMAND
ENGR. SECT. –APO 290
17 November 1945

Dear Mr. and Mrs. Glauber,

About two weeks ago it occurred to me that Mrs. Mayer had left Vienna for Shanghai and that Gerti, the Weiners, and you would be interested to hear about her. I found out easily where she had moved to and looked her up a few days later. She was rather surprised when an American officer left his jeep and asked for her, but soon everything was explained, and a long conversation about the various relatives and friends developed.

Today I was out there for lunch and I hurry now to transmit the received letter and to add a few personal observations. I would imagine that the enclosed letter gives a clear picture, but without knowing its contents, I would like to say that Mrs. Mayer looks well and gives the impression of great mental and physical activity. Very different from many people I have met in the same vicinity. She is still looking forward to better days and tries to display a gay and positive attitude towards life, and she entertained me with her many quick and extremely witty remarks. I hope you do not misunderstand these observations—I'm simply trying to answer the questions you must have about her life, impressions, surroundings, etc. She lives in her own small room in a simple, but well constructed, two-story building and is in steady contact with about twenty other Viennese people who seem to be members of this small, mutual-assistance community. The spirit there is a good one, very much different from the one I have found in the Hongkew Camps, where especially older people have lost hope, understanding, and decency.

Mrs. Mayer asked repeatedly if Rudy had moved to the coast because of his health, and I tried to convince her that it was only one of the reasons but that he is much happier now and feels perfectly all right also. I informed her about the contents of your letter, which had reached me two days before, after I had visited her for the first time. She strictly rejected any financial help and assured me of having enough money for many months to come. Nor does she want any parcels, though some white sugar, coffee, good canned food, etc. would be a good idea in my opinion. Whatever she needs through our PX she'll gladly get—otherwise I suggest that you send your mail through me, which should be much quicker.

Yours,
Gerhard K.

23 November 1945

From Erna Mayer

All my dearest ones,

I was delighted to receive your dear letters, one addressed to Gerhard Karplus and one addressed to me, dated 27 October. They arrived on the seventeenth, as well as the one sent via HICEM that arrived on the twenty-first. I just cannot tell you how happy I am to resume direct contact with you. That helps me survive the waiting period. Gerhard was so particularly nice. He visited me before the letter from you, dear Gusti, had arrived; that action was so very kind on his part. Last Saturday he was here for a meal, and promised to contact me again before the end of the following week. So now I hope to see him again very soon. When he is with me, I feel as close to him as if he were my near relative! And he has been telling me a lot about you. So now I am extremely curious, and just can't stop listening to him. But he is extremely busy and has to carry out his responsibilities. I am so very grateful that he has become so close to me, but I really lack nothing. I feel so well off financially that I have refused to take money from the Joint. Engel is utterly insistent that I should borrow money from him. He would like to have some of his money in the United States in order to avoid any international currency exchange restrictions. And, as I have requested in the past, please don't send me any money. And please, no more packages. They will cause you extra efforts and expenditures. One can buy pretty much anything here, if one wants to spend money.

Now first I want to answer all your questions. First of all, I want to correct the impression that we didn't have a visa in 1941. We had been at the consulate where they told us that it was now our turn and had made a medical appointment for us for 11 December.[73] And that was all that happened. But even if we had the visa already, the local

---

73   Pearl Harbor was bombed on December 7, 1941 ending all possibility of emigration from occupied China to the United States.

newspapers carried the news that all visas had been invalidated, and that everyone would have to start over again. So please do understand my current situation and keep it in mind. I have already visited the consulate, but their visa application process is not operational yet. Mr. Fuchs, who had another apartment in our building, has written repeatedly. He was one of the people who was most helpful with your dear poor father. He has been checking weekly at the consulate to see if anything is budging. I plan to omit nothing in my urgent quest to join all of you.

Now on to your question about the Hubers. They ran a very nice business on Bubbling Well Road. We met them through the Kardoses. We became so close to the Hubers that they even offered us some money. Your father was very nervous about our move to the Hongkew area. Mr. Huber didn't hesitate to lend us $400, without requiring any security from us. So they are some of the nicest and most accommodating people here in Shanghai. He was one of the most charitable people here before the Joint started to operate. In fact, he likes it very much when people mention his prior charity efforts. Poor Mrs. Kardos was the person who helped us get our apartment on Bubbling Well Road; she helped to care for your dear poor father for seven months. She passed away at the young age of fifty. Her son lives in England. This is a very sad story, but you cannot compare it to the European tragedy. That tragedy is so terrible that I cannot talk about it to you, dear Emil. I can only sob with you. It seems just so terrible that these events could have occurred to my poor sisters and sisters-in-law.[74] We are living here at the end of the earth, so such news dribbled in only very sparsely. We just didn't want to believe. And to our regret the rumors seemed to be paler than the cruel truth. Perhaps Father was very fortunate not to hear these news reports— they would have overwhelmed him. But what can we do now? Life continues— without the hope that I might join you in the future, life here would not be worthwhile for me. I always seem to reproach myself that I have been a bad human being. I have been saved, while

---

74   By this time Erna must have learned that Emil's parents and her sisters and sister-in-law had perished in the concentration camps.

all of them have perished. We did write to them often enough, telling them that they should try to come here. But regrettably they faced only obstacles. And that is what those criminals understood. But obviously there is no real purpose to write about them. Even though it seems so utterly difficult, we will have to find peace within ourselves. Life keeps going, but at least we can count on our young people—so let me congratulate all their parents. May these youngsters grow up in better times than their parents—our generation who had to suffer through such agony.

Dear Gusti, you wrote to us that Fred's wife had her third child. Is that Fred Glauber or Fritz-Fred Neubauer?[75] Let all of them be in good health, Amen! And I can recognize from your lines, dear Emil, that your daughter has grown up so much, and that Eleanor likes to go to dances. And that's really something! I have already said that I won't be able to see her until she gets married; probably she is gradually getting ready for adulthood. How do you feel about her growing up? The growing-up years seem to happen very fast. It seems very nice that Fred lives next door. Any news about Susi's parents? I am assuming that Maju was in such poor health that she didn't have to suffer through all the worst times. We have received dear letters from all the relatives that I treasure, as well as from all the dear friends whom we have left behind. Please let me know if any of them have survived. You know how much I am eager for all the news. Dear Emil, I am very curious what your current occupation is. I am very sorry that you also have to work on Sundays. Perhaps you can make some other arrangements. You really need some rest. Nobody can take that type of stress. I am delighted that you are doing so well—I would just be very happy to relieve you of much of that extra work.

Nothing much to report about me personally: I have been eating and drinking, and even sleeping. Supposedly, I look much better now and have gained some weight. Since the temperature has dropped already I can eat again. Thanks be to God, we are having a very nice autumn—the most beautiful season here. I have bought a half-ton of coal so that I won't be cold during the winter.

---

75   Refers to Fred Neubauer.

So now let me end this letter. The next letter will go to the dear Weiners, but I wanted to first answer the questions in your letter. Actually I have usually written a weekly letter. God knows where these letters ended up! And why are you writing me in English? Just so I can learn more English? By the way, I am reading only English language books. But do as you will, since I do understand your letters in English.

For now all of you—including the Weiners and the other dear relatives should feel hugged and kissed by
your Mother

To the Rosensteins   in San Francisco

From Erna

13 December 1945

My dear ones,

Many thanks for your dear letter, which I really enjoyed. At least I
know that personally you are doing well. Normally every letter ar-
riving here describes a tragedy. You cannot get away from these sad
thoughts, how much evil those Nazi dogs inflicted on all of us. It
seems utterly useless to waste any words on those events, and we cannot regain our peace of mind; the pain will last forever. I am pleased
to hear that your parents are doing relatively well, a real stroke of
luck. The most miserable home here is much better for any of us
than having stayed in Austria. When you write to them, please convey our warmest regards to them. I am doing quite well health wise.
I have created a circle of friends here so that I can live with *zures*[76]
more easily. Working seems to be my best remedy. On 16 December it will be exactly one year since your uncle got sick. His greatest
regret was that he did not live long enough to rejoin his children.
Thanks be to God, at least we were here. I would like to give the
Kollmanns a chance to write to you. I would like to wish you the very
best; I hope to verify that fact in the very near future and in person!
All my love to you!

With my fondest love and kisses I keep thinking of you.
Your Aunt Erna

---

76   Troubles

The following two undated letters were written by Liesl Kollmann from Shanghai

My very dear Rosensteins,

I hope that you have already received my answer to your Red Cross
note. Now we can resume our regular exchange of letters with all
of our dear ones who have survived. I just read your letter to your
dear aunt. I have also read all the letters from Käthe and Gusti. They
contained many good news items, as well as some terribly sad news.
It seems just terrible that so many of your relatives, dear Ernst, are
no longer alive. I am also very afraid that dear Victor, a resident of
Amsterdam, may have met the same dire fate. We also found out
that Egon's aunts are no longer alive. One of them ate some rotten
food and then died of a resulting intestinal infection. Both ended up
in Theresienstadt.[77] The other one was deported to Poland and was
killed there. Both of Egon's brothers met in Bari[78] by sheer chance,
probably while both were fleeing. Now both are working there for
the British government. So far I have only Red Cross letters from
them; so we don't know anything else about them. The main thing is
that both of them are alive. On the other hand, there is absolutely no
news about Egon's mother. Earlier today there was a radio announce-
ment that this coming spring, people may return to Austria; there
will be a preferential quota for physicians, technical people, engineers, etc. I think that we will return, since Egon would be unable to
continue his career as a physician elsewhere, except by reestablish-
ing his qualifications in that other country. We also don't know if we
could stay here as white people.[79] And I have been unable to stand
the local climate—especially in the summer; I get injections to keep
my body healthy; right now I weigh fifty kilograms. Up to now we
had not planned to leave, but Egon lost his very nice office as a result
of a Japanese proclamation requiring us to move to Hongkew. The

77   A concentration camp near Prague in Czechoslovakia, also known as Terezin.
78   A seaport town in southeastern Italy
79   Some refugees stayed in Shanghai, even in Hongkew, for a few more years after the war
ended while they pursued visas and sponsors in other countries.

war in the Pacific also led to the loss of his American and British patients. We have been forced to live in a "designated area," that is in one of Shanghai's worst areas. So we just wanted to tell you this in brief. What kind of plans do you, our dear ones, have for the future? Do you want to remain where you are now, or will there be a time to see each other again? We hope that our dear aunt[80] will have an opportunity to report all our news from here. We are living in the same house with seven other families from Vienna. It is a real tragedy that our dear poor uncle could not rejoin you. All of us admired how Tante Erna performed the nursing care during his long illness, where she could not really sleep for many weeks; we were all afraid that she would be unable to survive that very difficult time. Thanks to her extremely strong will and her deep understanding she was able to summon all her strength to keep going. Now she looks very well again, and has only a single desire!

For now, my dear ones, we want to wish you the very best!

From Liesl Kollmann Shanghai
[Preceding page missing]

… that you are so satisfied, *toi toi toi*. [81] The same also applies to the dear Weiners and to the Rosensteins. Ernst has not changed at all; Trude has become a fashion plate, and applies lipstick to her lips. Lore has become a young lady, and is very good-looking. Now we are in the habit of saying that if Aunt Erna doesn't emigrate very soon, then she'll arrive just in time for her wedding! Hopefully she'll be able to make it much sooner—in our opinion her progress is just too slow, but the officials aren't in any hurry. The Chinese government seems to deem it quite important to get rid of these refugees by getting them repatriated. They have designated us as enemy aliens and consider us Austrians as being at the same social level as "Aryan"

---

80   Dear aunt refers to Erna
81   An expression to ward off bad luck: "knock on wood."

Germans.[82] Thanks to their long-term business connections and personal assets they will be allowed to keep on staying here. So therefore this prejudicial attitude seems to be directed only against the Jews. For example, Jewish physicians have received no licenses to practice here; furthermore, the local authorities insist that these physician applicants need to qualify in Chinese, absolutely impossible for any of these applicants. So we have not decided for sure, and things always seem to turn out differently than planned. But most likely we will have to return to Austria. That certainly would not be our hearts' desire since we will be unable to forget what those dogs have done to us in the past. Nor can we think of forgiving them for their misdeeds. But physicians seem to be very much in demand there. Egon could get a position there immediately to restart his private medical practice; he would not have to pass any professional examinations as he would have to do elsewhere. A newly arrived physician would have to wait five years before qualifying to practice in Australia and New Zealand; I think that this process would take two years in America. If this accursed Pacific War had not occurred we would have never considered returning to Austria. Egon's practice in Vienna would have evolved to serve a mainly elite group of patients, composed almost exclusively of foreigners. He would have practiced in an air-conditioned office located in a tall building. Instead, we are now looking at seven lost years, as well as facing the need to restart an entirely new medical practice. But there is one thing that I won't miss if we move away from here: the hot summers that I cannot cope with; usually I receive many shots to counteract the problems caused by the local summer heat. This experience seems to apply to most people of the white race.

Our dear aunt looks well again; her health really seemed to suffer from caring for poor Uncle because she never left his bedside, didn't get any sleep for many weeks, and responded very negatively when someone offered to relieve her. Only during Uncle's last night did she allow two gentlemen to take turns watching him. All of us were

---

82   The Chinese, who fought the Axis powers (Japan, Germany, & Italy), apparently chose to regard Austrian Jewish refugees as being identical to non-Jewish Germans, i.e. Axis citizens.

full of admiration for her since her care for Uncle Hans proved more than superhuman.

We have had no news from Fritz, except for a telegram that arrived a few days ago. It contained only the query as to which currency he should use for a deposit to our account. Our letter is in the mail to him, with the hope that everybody is healthy; now we eagerly await a letter with lots of details. To be honest, I still have very little hope that we can expect a sign of life from Victor. He was in the Netherlands where the Jews were subject to the same cruel treatment wherever the Nazi criminals went. But perhaps we may get some news from him sometime in the future. Thank God, Egon's brothers are alive; they met accidentally in Bari after apparently fleeing. Now they are working for the British government; we only have some letters from the Red Cross, and thus know nothing more about them. They wrote absolutely nothing about Egon's mother; she had been in Yugoslavia. The very same trouble seems to prevail continuously everywhere! Just remember how nice it was when we enjoyed our last joint ski trips; our main worry was whether there would be enough snow on Sunday! (Of course, we also had a few other worries.) We would like to thank you, dear Rosensteins, for your kind offer to send us an affidavit; that seems like a very kind and considerate gesture on your part. But we cannot really make up our minds to come to the United States because of the long period of study needed to pass the U.S. medical examinations. Who knows if Gonni[83] could work in a hospital in the meantime. After all, you need some kind of income to live there. I would accept any type of job offered to me. But I believe that we are no longer young and spry enough. We could have done that seven years ago, but then that just wasn't an option for us. We have heard that Egon's colleagues—mainly other physicians—are doing very well in the United States; Dr. Weizenberg and Dr. Weissmann (both in New York) are earning between $1,500 and $2,000 (and sometimes even more) per month. They seem to work very hard, but it pays off with that very good income. We frequently

---

83   Egon Kollmann. The Kollmanns did settle in San Francisco.

meet Dr. and Mrs. Herzog. We spent a very nice Christmas Eve at their home.

So let me finish up for today. Hopefully we can look forward to hearing nice news from you.

Warmest regards from
Your Liesl

I am absolutely delighted that you are doing so well and are so successful!
Yours Egon

31 December 1945

From Erna

All my very dearest ones,

So here it is New Year's Eve and I can't do anything better than to do a little bit of schmoozing with you, my very dearest ones. What I wish for you and me is that the Almighty will listen to all of us to hear our plea to be reunited again! Amen! Let all of you be healthy, and may all of your endeavors achieve success! Amen! For the past several years your father and I have wished for nothing else except to be reunited with you again. To our regret he did not live to have this sincerest desire fulfilled—that thought will sadden me forever. Just one year ago I was absolutely convinced that his good health would return. Oh what regrets! But I just don't want to keep crying in front of you, nor burden you with my personal problems more than absolutely necessary. When I returned home earlier this afternoon I found your letter, dear Käthe, with the postscript from dear Agnes. That letter made it a real holiday for me with all your news. But, dear Käthe, you are utterly wrong in thinking that I am disapproving of you just because you are still in bed at 10. I am quite certain that this normally doesn't happen; instead I am assuming that you really needed the rest so urgently. I am already looking forward to being able to serve you breakfast in bed! And you, dear Rudy, as well as the dear Glaubers, will be completely surprised how much I have changed. I just wish that I could spoil you in person! On 3 January I plan to visit the consulate; I am going to ask Gerhard Karplus to go with me. He came here for a meal last Saturday and I was overjoyed to have him join me. The affidavit papers have arrived; I am really very sorry that you have been subjected to the double effort and expense. I guess that I should have confirmed the receipt by a telephone call. But obviously such a call would not have really helped. The expected packages have not arrived so far; I will confirm their arrival when received. Just for your information, here American coffee currently costs one dollar per pound. I suspect that coffee is not much cheaper for you. I am sure that Gerhard will tell you that I lack for nothing here. Yesterday, Sunday, I had my normal guests, Mr. Fuchs and Mrs. Boeckbinder. I served them ground beef with steamed cabbage and potatoes, and Semmelauflauf.[84] I hope that you will approve of this menu. During the past month I spent $23—hopefully, not too little in your opinion.

So now I have another special request; I hope that you, dear Gusti, can take care of this matter. Please don't be mad at me, and I know that you are more than busy. But Mrs. Kriegl nee Vlcek, my neighbor, asked me for this favor, and I would really like to help her out. As I have written you repeatedly, she is a Christian lady who still has her parents in Vienna. She is very worried about them, so she would like to send them some food items with your help, if possible. I am including a separate small piece of paper with the Viennese address. Right now, Mrs. Kriegl doesn't know if they still reside in that apartment, but has written to her sister in Vienna about the address. The package should be sent to this sister for forwarding to her parents and her sisters.

Liese Sedlarik on behalf of Emanuel Klein, Vienna 21, Deublergasse 18

They are genuinely Christian, even though the name sounds Jewish. The old gentleman worked for a locomotive manufacturing firm for many years. If possible, please include the following food items:

2 lbs of butter, 3 lbs of meat, 1 lb of cheese, 1 lb of coffee, 1 lb of condensed milk, 1 lb of chocolate, 1 lb of candy

We don't know if you are allowed to send such a package to Vienna nor what you can spend for this package. If you, dear Gusti, feel some suitable substitute food may be better, feel free to choose that. Please write me the total cost and I will get the equivalent money here, just a simple exchange of funds. Please be sure to include the cost for packing and shipping. The people here know that such a shipment will run into some money, but, dear Gusti, please don't feel any constraints. So that completes the special request.

---

84   A bread pudding made with rolls and eggs.

Gerhard also brought me Paul's letter with its very sad contents. Those poor people really seem to have gone though a lot of hardships. They were really very brave! But as for those of us here, we certainly did not live in paradise, and we have also lived through a lot—what a lot of grief here! There still is a strong anti-Semitic trend here right now; rumors have it that the local anti-Jewish proclamation is to be lifted very soon, presumably due to U.S. pressure. But you must not concede anything here because otherwise you lose face. It is just so very sad that anti-Semitism still persists even after the end of the terrible war. Here the local German refugees love to take walks, have lots of money, and the very few that are in camp[85] seem to be doing very well.

Katinka, I am perfectly comfortable with your writing style when your writing is so spontaneous. I was so sorry to learn from Paul's letter that you, dear Rudy, are suffering from another bout with bronchitis. Hopefully you should be okay again by now. It seems to be an absolute miracle that Ernst Kaufmann is still alive. I am very sorry to hear that Paul Hirschhaeuter and Hohenberg didn't have a chance to meet. They appear to have received my letter to Vienna sent in May where I reported your father's death. Today Mr. Wodicka received a Red Cross letter from a former female employee that she has been running his business; she asked him to send a power of attorney and come back to Vienna as soon as possible. Please write to me what would be best to include in such a power of attorney, as well as its appropriate wording. So now I will await your instructions in this matter. Dear Käthe, I have to disappoint you about my comforter: I cannot stitch one from scratch, but only mend it a little. I plan to bring two old comforters with me that I still own, but you need to arrange to have two new ones made. I am delighted to hear that Henry and Helen[86] are learning to play the piano, but—thanks be to God—have not inherited my musical talents. Fritz Duldner's wife, Hella, a music teacher, is curious to know how long the children have been learning piano, as well as what pieces they are playing. Presumably they have a refugee serving them as their teacher. How much do you

85   Probably refers to the Hongkew area.
86   Käthe's children Americanized their names: Otto to Henry later Hank; Liesl, Liese Lene to Helen.

103

pay for an hourly lesson? At this point I have already decided their son Kurt should marry Lore. Mrs. Duldner has already declared her love for her prospective daughter-in-law! It doesn't really take too much imagination for that development! About six weeks ago her older son married a Chinese woman—they were not very pleased with that marriage, but had to get used to that fact.

I am now continuing this letter on 2 January. Yesterday several visitors came: Dr. and Mrs. Sachs, Mr. and Mrs. Nanseck, and Mrs. Buchstab. All of them were very attentive to me by bringing flowers, cookies, and some canned goods. I really don't like to receive such gifts, but I cannot keep them from doing so. Just recently many wonderful cans of surplus UNRRA[87] food items were distributed here. That was really a grandiose charitable act; it results in all local people being fed much better than before. Tomorrow I plan to visit the consulate again; I will let you know about the results by means of a letter to be mailed by Gerhard Karplus. So there is nothing else new to report for today

Stay well and feel kissed by your   Mother

Dear Gusterl,

January 19 is in the very future; I assume that this letter will arrive in a timely fashion. Here's a particularly impressive birthday kiss. I'll go light on the birthday wishes! May God fulfill all your wishes. And also send birthday congratulations to Trude!

[Handwritten lines]
My dear ones,

Made absolutely no progress at the consulate because I had to register from scratch again. I need to mail the completed forms to them. Only then will they notify me as to when I can leave for the United States. So I have to keep on waiting. Regrettably, Gerhard couldn't come here. Kisses   Mother

---

87   United Nations Relief and Rehabilitation Administration

9 January 1946   New York

From Gusti Glauber to Schwarz

[In response to his letter of October/November 1945]

Dear Mr. Engineer Schwarz!

You seem to be especially nice and considerate to write such a kind and well-meaning letter to us that concerns our very dear mother. We are very, very grateful to you for doing so. Obviously, you can imagine that we are extremely proud that Mutti is doing so well health-wise that she can accomplish all the things she does. We would love to have had her here with us as of yesterday. You can certainly imagine that feeling on our part. We have done absolutely everything that we could do from here. And, of course, we can only continue to hope for the very best for her. But first of all we need to assume that she will receive her visa very soon so that she can join us here after an ocean or airline trip.

Quite obviously, you are very correct in describing Mutti's suffering, hard work, and other problem situations. But we feel absolutely powerless to do anything for her, except to try hard to convince her to give up working. She should worry only about her personal life. As you wrote, she will have to undergo a physical exam at the American consulate, and therefore needs to be in an excellent state of health; otherwise she will have major difficulties in reaching the United States very soon. As we have heard from Mutti, thanks be to God, Mrs. Engel is doing much better now so that Mutti's help and regular visits should no longer be necessary. And why on earth does she go to her so early in the morning? I thought that Mutti's visits would start around ten and end around two, as is customary here. And for that people pay about $4.50, or even more! And, God knows, some of these ladies don't even show up all the time!

We are most interested in what you have written about Mutti's life—that is in sharp contrast to what she writes to us. Every letter talks about how well all her friends have treated her and our father. We are just very sorry that this wonderful and good gentleman did not live long enough to be reunited with us.

We are delighted that you are doing so well. But we also read in the newspapers that Shanghai's authorities are planning to expel the Jewish refugees in the near future, but we anticipate that they cannot carry out this plan in a hurry. Therefore, whenever Shanghai's economy eventually returns to its former state then its residents will be able to earn a good living again. But the difficult climate is a wholly different matter. After all, we did not leave Austria because of its climate. Here the climate is also not very nice; sometimes we have all four seasons within a single day! But you get used to the local climate, except for the humidity during the summers that really tires you out. And then you need to consider New York City with its rush and the huge distances that make life here extremely stressful. So Emil urgently needs a vacation after our many stressful years, but he just cannot spare the time!

Dear Mr. Engineer, I sincerely thank you for all the good that you are doing for our dear mother. Please don't worry about her refusal to borrow any money from you; maybe she will in the future. Mutti always writes that she has everything she needs, so I don't know what she really still needs. And please don't complain about our sending occasional packages to you; we love to do it. After all, you have very good friends who hopefully will enjoy them. They really are not that expensive.

Very hearty regards! And we wish you lots of luck in all of your endeavors!

9 January 1946   New York

From Gusti Glauber to Erna

My very dear Mother,

I am overjoyed to confirm the receipt of your dear letter dated December 23, 1945. Gerhard Karplus's help has made everything move much faster. I am truly extremely grateful that he has been so very good and so very helpful to us. Regrettably, I have been unable to visit his wife, Gerti. She simply cannot be reached by telephone, so occasionally I write to her. Dear Mother, you are so considerate to number your letters. But some of them seem to get lost. We don't have number 4 or 5. But I don't remember the sequence numbers of my letters. It seems simpler to remember the dates. Just now a friend called me from Cleveland, all worried that I hadn't written to her for two weeks! So therefore she assumed that something was wrong here; that's what you call real affection! These people seem to be well off, and therefore use the telephone very frequently.

In Cleveland we really had such extremely good friends on whom we could always rely. That really means a lot. I am so very glad that the affidavits have finally arrived. Now we are very eager to hear about some successful results at the consulate. But now I am beginning to think that you, my dear Mother, should stop working—we cannot be sufficiently grateful to our dear Lord that He has kept you healthy up to now; and He also gave you the strength to survive these very difficult and tough years so that you still have the strength to write these wonderful letters. They do prove conclusively that you—at your advanced age—are still so full of energy and persistence. We are so terribly proud of you; and we hope and pray that you will remain healthy and will continue to take care of yourself. After all, you need to undergo—and pass—a medical examination at the consulate. You know very well that we can offer you only some limited advice. In any case we expect you to do what you are intent on doing. And we would be very pleased if you stopped working, so you can take care of all the things that you need to do and be ready to travel on the spur of the moment. Some acquaintances were supposed to leave by plane from Lisbon. They had to get ready for their departure within twenty minutes! They happened to be in a coffeehouse and they actually managed that feat! I only wish that you were already at that stage. I am also of the opinion that you should sell everything that you don't absolutely need. Perhaps, if you are going to fly, then you will need an airline suitcase; if you are going by ship, you'll have to struggle during the trip. After all, anything you may need is available here. Some of your current possessions may be too costly to take along. I am absolutely delighted to do anything that we can do for you.

We were delighted with Mr. Engineer Schwarz's letter. It is very touching how concerned he is with your well-being. And probably he is essentially quite correct about your situation with Mrs. Engel. But dear Mother, please remember that our sincerest wish is to be together with you for many, many years. Why should you scrub her floors when that is not really necessary, and when their apartment is not heated properly? We just don't understand the need for you to help Mrs. Engel, nor why you are slaving away there. A friend of the Schnitzers, Mr. Por, a Hungarian gentleman, has lived in Shanghai for twenty-five years; his wife was born there. He is planning a business trip from here to Shanghai next January. I would love to send you some things if I only knew what you need. Please don't be mad at us about the packages that have not arrived so far. Feel free to give away any items that you don't need. Gerhard wrote us that he visited the hospital to help some of the patients. You can donate some of the unneeded items to them. You can do what you want to. Later this week Susie will send you a package. We get along with that family splendidly.

The following two letters were missing the first pages.

January 1946—

From Erna

I hope that you will not be mad at me if I sell some of the contents of your parcel, for example the stockings. Here they are a very sought-after item. I wear only black ones, and furthermore I have an ample supply. In addition some razor blades, cotton thread, and powdered milk (three pounds of it); I prefer to drink my coffee black. I can just hear you say, "This mother is just incorrigible!" But you really will not have to stuff me; actually I am gaining some weight! I have more than enough stockings, clothes, coats—in fact, I am just in the process of selling some extra underwear! Here you can find customers for everything! I am utterly amazed not to hear anything from England; please send me their addresses so I can write to them in the near future.[88]

Gerhard has just left me; so now I can continue this letter. I did get your letters, one from dear Gusti dated 28 December and one from dear Käthe dated 24 December. So Gerhard will fly away for about fourteen days; I assume that he will return with a load of letters from you. He did promise me that his secretary, Miss Teltscher, would continue to help me. Yesterday her father was kind enough to help me with my mail by bringing me the letters from the Weiners and the Glaubers. I don't know how this arrangement will work in the future. I plan to write to you even if I don't receive any letters from you. I miss your letters as much as I miss all of you.

Now to give answers to the questions in your letters. I have already told you about my status at the U.S. consulate. Just like all the others here, I had to restart the registration process from scratch, but supposedly the preexisting quota status is expected to remain. I provided all the needed information to them. Currently there are only vice-consular officers here. When Gerhard returns he plans to go to

88   Erna's nieces and nephew and their families had escaped to England before 1941.

the consulate with me. Now we just have to give the consulate some time, since they have had to reregister thousands of people.[89] As long as my case is in the pipeline, any effort to speed it up probably would be fruitless. All the needed paperwork has arrived; in fact, the papers from the dear Glaubers came twice. I am of the opinion and firmly convinced that none of the needed papers is missing, and the affidavits are still within their time limits. As to what I am supposed to bring along, I would like to sell all my bed linens and bedding, but I want to do that exactly as you, dear Käthe suggest. I will not have enough hand baggage. If I go by boat then the large suitcases will not cost me extra. I do own coats and dresses, though they are no longer fashionable, but they are in a satisfactory state; replacing them over there probably would cost a lot of money. I still own a good fur liner; luckily I sold my fur jacket in 1943. I just was not in the mood to run around Hongkew in such a fancy outfit. I sold it for 5,500 Shanghai dollars. And replaced it with a thirty-nine-year-old jacket for US $55. I thought that was a good trade at that time. By the way, any fancy fur coat tends to get ruined by the local climate; therefore, your father could not see any objections to my coat exchange. If I take the huge ship suitcase with me then it can hold my comforter and some pillows. Since the relevant bed linens are already over there this idea seems okay.

---

89   It is estimated that twenty thousand Jews entered Shanghai between 1939 and 1941.

[First page missing]

[January 1946]

Dear Katinka, I'll be able to recognize your children, but there is very little chance that they will recognize me! But that situation won't last for very long! It is nice to know that you don't live too far from Agnes, Felix, and family, and the Rosensteins. I would love to catch up with everybody in the *mishpoche*,[90] something that I have missed for the past several years. Dear Rudy, how is your asthma? I hope that it's gone or bothers you only rarely! Dear Käthe, please don't worry about my malaria. Obviously, I started to take Atabrine when it first hit me; you are not supposed to get any more malaria attacks thereafter. At least that's what it says on the label, but I still have had malaria attacks in March, April, and May. At the insistence of our local community council I consulted Dr. Spaniermann, who ordered a complete sequence of quinine and Atabrine tablets for me. Since then I have had no more malaria attacks, *toi toi toi*—a complete cure.

So now it's your turn, my dear Glaubers. I hope that you have spent the holidays well. I am very sorry to hear that you, dear Emil, didn't get much of a rest. I really believe that you enjoyed your visit with Vilma[91] and her daughter. It's a real pleasure to hug such a little kid! I am quite certain that she has inherited her sunny disposition from her father, Hans, who was always laughing.

I want to complete the power of attorney even though your letter didn't clarify exactly what you needed. In any case, I am sending each of you a notarized photocopy of your father's death certificate. When I complete all these forms, I plan to send them to Hans Adler. But I still don't know whose name should appear on the power of attorney for the Pilsen case; therefore, I am still waiting for your instructions. Now we are also starting to receive news from Vienna. It appears that the city probably was quite heavily damaged. The sister-in-law of Mr. Engel's Christian wife wrote us that many local Nazis were

90   Yiddish for relatives
91   Vilma and Hans Adler were cousins of Emil. They settled in Washington, D.C.

allowed to keep their very nice government positions—after all, they were not real Nazis, but were forced to wear Nazi swastikas on their lapels! Just earlier today I visited the Posamentiers. Currently she needs to stay in bed due to some inflamed veins; she did ask about the Koenigsteins. I plan to talk to her tomorrow about what you, dear Gusti, just wrote me.

I'm glad that you have received Schwarz's reimbursement; I am delighted that he has repaid you so that I can lend him some more money when he needs it. The old gentleman is in pretty bad physical shape; therefore, it is very questionable whether he will survive long enough to see his son again.

Gerhard mentioned to me, his wife, Gerti, has been in a hospital for some sort of surgery; now she is doing well again. That's why you, dear Gusti, could not reach her. I think you can continue writing to Gerhard until you are notified that he has returned home. He is extremely nice; he has even offered to help me at no cost when I move. Right now everything is just so expensive! Dear Gucki, just don't worry about me! I am living very decently and have about three hundred dollars in savings. Since I am always selling something, I still don't need to touch these savings. And of course, the Schwarzes and the Engels will give me some money if necessary; after all, they prefer to have all that money waiting for them over there! So please don't send me anything! I know in the depth of my soul that I have the very best children! But I just can't use anything else, and I have more than enough to *nosh* on here.

I plan to look personally for Mr. Quartiermeister since I pass his home every day; I plan to invite him to my home and then tell him everything. Mr. Engineer Schwarz also knows him, as does Mr. Kisch. Mr. Kisch is about to visit Mr. Schwarz tomorrow and plans to invite Mr. Quartiermeister to visit me. By the way, to whom is Dorli engaged? After all, she is still very young. I would guess around nineteen. I am delighted to know that you have received the Chinese pajamas. Then you, dear Emil, probably also got the woolen underwear and the tuxedo.

Mrs. Kriegl just bought a Linzer torte again. I have donated one pudding to each of my eight fellow tenants—everybody was delighted with their gift. Mrs. Kriegl is especially grateful that you sent the food parcels to her parents in Vienna; please continue doing that if you want to do so. Dear Gusti, please send these parcels only if you get paid for them as if this was a business transaction! Please send my warmest congratulations to Martha Gruener—she is one of the few people who have now been united with their children! How is Egon doing? Does Lotte earn some money on her own? After Proclamation 43[92] we received a telegram from the Lichtmanns, which we have already answered. Furthermore, Mr. Schwarzbart gave us the equivalent of one hundred dollars in local currency, at one third of the value. Did Mr. Schwarzbart come from Pilsen? We also got some news about Herbert, including once via Spain. We always answered him. Mrs. Buchstab just left me, a very boring person. I just can't do anything about that, but she really likes me without my liking her! She made me an offer of a small room in her apartment if I cannot find something else. So you can see that I won't end up on the street! Supposedly she had been Victor Schratter's friend; she also would like to know the address of Otto Schratter or his mother. Perhaps Gerti has that information. Her husband passed away two years ago. While they seemed to have brought along many valuable things, her husband insisted on skimping on food. My Dukatenbuchterl[93] made a big hit with her since they didn't cost her anything. Admittedly, I sound pretty annoyed with her, but that's my personal feeling for her! Incidentally, she is one of Egon's patients who is just getting a suntan treatment; so I am just making a sacrifice for one of his relatives.

I have already offered my opinion about flying. I am not afraid of flying but I would like to avoid it because of the much greater expense, as well as because of the need to travel with only very few suitcases. I am not doing anything through the Joint. If I were to meet the chief god on the street, I would take off my hat and hold it very low while bowing.

I can't seem to wait until my time to greet you all again in person!

Many kisses   Your Mother

---

92   The order to move to Hongkew. See footnote 55.
93   Fried cakes that look like ducat coins

16 February 1946

All my very dearest,

Yesterday was truly a very special day: six letters arrived all at once—that's really quite a red-letter event! Yours arrived by airmail, one from dear George who seems to be a "golden boy," one from Paul Schoenmann, a dear letter dated 4 February from the Weiners, one from Olga Deutschland, and one from Emil Taussig. Also received an issue of the Aufbau[94] as well as some newspapers published in December and January. Many, many thanks for all that stuff—so now I have plenty of reading material. I just don't have any patience for books. A ship just came in; therefore much mail has arrived. Thanks be to God. As I have been saying all along, I live on letters and pictures. Everybody is telling me that I look extremely well; the same people used to tell me that I didn't look too well.

Dear Emil, I would like to heed your advice to come by plane. But please look for a job for me so that I can earn the difference in travel cost. But I think that I will be disappointing you: I have aged a lot. I am not tired, but I have become far less enterprising. Perhaps I will have the chance to observe what others in my age range are doing.

Mawei is really a fantastic person because I remember how spoiled she was in Vienna. It would be just wonderful to meet her in New York! I wonder if I will be in the United States in time to attend the boys' Bar Mitzvahs. Perhaps I can make it for George's, but probably not for Henry's, even though I really want to attend. Many thanks to the Weiners for the very nice picture of you in front of your fireplace. That scene looks very homelike. At first, I could not understand the attached card, but on Saturday Gerhard immediately recognized this kind of card where the explanation is on the back. I have an ample supply of everything I need, and truly lack for nothing. You can buy lots of butter here, both locally produced and Australian butter. Dear Gusti, did you already mail a package to me? Please be sure to write down what you spent for me—I can repay you immediately. The Engels want to apologize to you for bothering you to pay that small

94   A German-Jewish newspaper that was very popular among the Jewish refugees

amount to Mrs. Liane Latzke. They arranged to have a package sent to her sister-in-law in Vienna, and therefore wanted to repay that expense. By the way, this lady's late husband was one of my acquaintances of my teen years, as well as a good friend of Uncle Pepi. The world is really small! Mrs. Wodicka asked me to pay a short visit to her. Two lady friends were there when the name Willi Halpern was mentioned. Of course I pointed out that I knew Mr. Halpern. Dear Emil, do you know him? He used to own a diamond-polishing firm. And does that tie into the textile business? It is just so amazing how people have changed their business careers. I was quite saddened by hearing about the news of poor Will; I just can't express my sympathy for both of them. But it will be plain luck when Fritz comes back. At least then she will get some relief from his presence since she is so desperately ill. Some time ago Irma had the same illness and died from it at age eighteen. She was with us when she was a newlywed and was receiving radiation treatments. We can only say that she was a poor dear.

When I look at your pictures and those of your homes, the contrast is huge between here and the United States. But apparently the majority of the people here live this way; therefore these differences are not really obvious to them. You, dear Käthe, have a built-in heater. Here we have iron stoves in our rooms where the pipes traverse the room and then go through a window. Naturally, any wind comes through the window and chills the room. Gerhard was very delighted to know that you really like where you live. He brought me some pictures of your homes that looked just wonderful. Sad to say, he is very lonesome, but he is considered essential and thus has no real hope for going home in the near future. Gusti, please don't send him any film. He has no time for photography. But I turned spendthrift and had Professor Schiebert take a picture of me. Tomorrow Mr. Kriegl, my neighbor, will also snap my picture. Here photography is not very popular because it is too expensive. By the way, Gerhard flew to Manila for a few days; he'll let me know when he returns. He has also talked about relocating me, but he is bound to forget about that idea, and I won't remind him. In any case you can continue sending my mail through him. His secretary knows about this method; she lives nearby and delivers these letters to me in his absence.

Yesterday I served pot roast with rice and brussels sprouts; Topfenbuchteln[95] were the dessert. Apparently he especially liked the dessert. This morning when I met my neighbor Mrs. Franken Busch, she told me immediately that she had heard how wonderful that dessert had been! Gerhard visits her regularly. She is a née Bielitz and used to be at Altmanns. Her late husband died heavily indebted, but she paid off all the outstanding amounts subsequently; she is extremely capable even though she is somewhat crippled due to polio. Gusti, you have asked me if I need some clothes. Please don't send anything. After all, you want me to travel with minimal baggage; so why should I get some more clothes? I am just used to owning very few clothes. Here you don't need anything! The same thing is true for the apartment. You become sloppier as time goes by. For example, starting with the first summer I have not worn a foundation garment. You just can't wear one during the local summers; so I have just gotten used to not wearing one on a year-round basis. I have also forgotten what it is to take a bath. For the past three years we have lived in a type of garbage dump, and we have to thank the good Lord that we were able to live that well. We only become aware of this situation when we can communicate with the outside world. You seem to have received the power of attorney; anything you can do on my behalf will be just fine with me. I am very sorry that Karl is suffering in Czechoslovakia. Is it difficult to get a job there? If the U.S. consulate there operates as slowly as here, then he'll have to wait for a long while. I am assuming that nothing can be done here without the permit from Philadelphia. But let's hope that it will arrive here in the near future. Is there still no news about Richard?[96] Does he want to stay in Palestine? You have never met his wife. Was that the reason for the divorce? A Mrs. Binder-Delikat asked about Mrs. Fischer; can you pass this query on to her? Otherwise nothing else is new here. I am continuing to live here, carry on as usual, and

---

95   Pan rolls stuffed with pot cheese
96   Emil's brother.

stay at the Engels to make my sad life easier to bear, and they don't mind my staying out late. If you want to offer any comments about my acquaintances, please use a separate piece of paper. They are really controlling me right now, and don't want to miss reading any of my letters. Otherwise, everyone is very nice to one another, except for Mrs. Dr. Eitelberg—she is very nervous and is now at odds with Luscha Duldner. I just hope that I won't get into a fight with her. But apparently she has a lot of respect for me, and I know quite well how to deal with her.

Of course, there is a lot to talk about, but when I write to you about everything there is just nothing to add at the end of my letter. Dear Käthe, your letter mentioned the Raubitscheks, who are supposed to have friends here. That may be very true, but I don't know them. Actually, I am not meeting too many people here. Many people know me, but generally I don't know them. The day before yesterday I visited Mrs. Lion, who is from Germany. She used to travel with us—that's just a memory for me. Her siblings live in Forest Hills; her son is in the U.S. Army. So she is looking forward to meeting me again in the United States.

So now let me end this letter for today. Now I am going to wash myself with holy water after not having enough hot water. That's what we call that substitute for a bath.

Continued on February 18

Actually nothing more worth reporting has happened since yesterday. Marianne Stern called to tell me that she had received her affidavit from Puzzi; she plans to visit me later this week for a schmooze. Dear Rudy, I am delighted to hear that you have found such a well-paying job. I can imagine that you can use the extra money so very well. Naturally roof repairs are very expensive—those are the joys of homeownership. But in any case, you are having this work done for your personal benefit. I am curious if you, dear Käthe, also got a raise, or if you switched jobs. I am very sorry to hear that you are working so very hard. When the good Lord allows me to join you in the near future, I would love to relieve you of many of your chores. But just let everyone be healthy! Dear Rudy, how is your asthma doing? I hope that you have found some relief from it. I am delighted that Trude Steiner is doing so well, and that you get along so well with her. Dear Käthe, I hope that your patients will consider you God's angel. Some time ago Mr. Engel helped the Josephs financially; supposedly their children have repaid that money. In this sense Mr. Engel is exceptionally charitable—he offered them the money just on our personal assurance that they were very decent people.

I believe that I have answered all your questions. Now I still want to write to all my grandchildren. Will they laugh a lot at me, that is, my poor English! Never mind![97] I don't let anybody else correct my letters, nor let anyone else write them for me. I just can't do it any better! Dear Emil, how well did your expense accounts work out with your firm? Are you planning to travel to Brazil and Peru? In any case it seems quite nice to have the opportunity to take such trips. But such a trip also involves a lot of responsibility and stress. In my thoughts I am really living with you and participating in your lives.

Stay healthy and feel kissed and hugged by your,   Mother

---

97   Never mind! is written in English

[Original in English]

27 February 1946

To Henry and Helen

My dear grandchildren,

With your sweet letters I have great joy, also with the nice pictures. But your signature dear Henry I doesn't can read. Is this your name at the scouts? What are you doing the whole day? Have you much to do with your newspaper or have you one other job? Are you now learning for the Barmizwah? I were very happy if I can be in this time at you. And you dear Helen got you one nice report card? What for gifts you got to Christmas? This you have forgot to wrote me and I have so great interest for all concerning you. Got you sometimes letters from grandmother Bertha? If you write to her, I send her my hearty greetings. I send today to your parents one photo of mine. I am curious if you Henry can little remember of the grandmother. But never mind if I saw you the last time this is nearly eight years and you was a small boy. Now we got one fresh wintertime and it is cold and windy. Next month I have to move in one other place. I hope you are both well and are good learning in the school.

Many many kisses and love.
Your grandmother

Erna in Shanghai 1946

5 March 1946

My dear ones,

Earlier today I went to the consulate to check if that document had arrived yet from Philadelphia, but it had not. We cannot do anything at this end. I am very downhearted that nothing is budging, even though various other people are already setting up their moves. I was really very surprised during my visit to the consulate when I ran into Walter Immergut, Nellie's husband (nee Bleier); he is also Hans Bleier's brother-in-law. He can tell you that I look very well and also feel quite healthy. Please do help Mr. Immergut if you can. He would love to have his son attend school there. Perhaps Felix may be able to help him. Mr. Immergut has only a U.S. transit visa since he plans to travel to Colombia. Essentially, please help him with his lodging so that his housing costs will be minimal. I am writing this letter at Nellie's office; therefore I need to keep it short.

All my love and many kisses
Your old Mother

17 March 1946

My beloved dearest ones,

I think that I have confirmed the receipt of all your letters, but I am not entirely clear because my move has left me in a sort of confused state. So I did move yesterday; now I am living in a very pleasant three-room apartment, with all the comforts of life. Schwarz arranged to have everything redecorated at very great expense, but I am very pleased with the results.

Now I am living very centrally in the French area, but I didn't care where the place was actually located—I would have liked it best if I had been able to leave our stable for a ship cabin. Tomorrow more than forty lucky people are leaving for Australia. That's a truly wonderful idea, with UNRRA picking up all the expenses; many of the prior immigrants are already doing very well over there. For example, the son of the butcher Bauer has already made so much money that he could buy his own home with a swimming pool. All that happened even though UNRRA paid the entire cost of the moves. What should I do if my move would have to depend on UNRRA? But there is no current chance for leaving Shanghai. UNRRA is trying very hard to move us refugees away from here.

Last Friday I was invited to a meeting at the Joint. As I had expected, they asked me about repaying my outstanding loans to them. In summary, I, that is, we, owe them about 573 Swiss francs, and they wanted me to pay them $160[98] on the spot. We agreed on a compromise amount of $150, which I paid to them on that very day. I hope that you agree with my action. UNRRA doesn't want to accept partial repayments if they know that this person's children are doing well financially. I do hope that you will agree with how I handled this situation. It seems that we don't have to repay food money, but we just aren't the type of people who want to depend on charity. I made the repayment so promptly because I was still living in Hongkew and didn't have to wait for my appointment. Otherwise I would

---

98      $160 in 1946 would equal about $1,650 in 2006.

have had to spend more time on this matter. Nowadays, when I visit Hongkew, I am so popular that I have to schmooze with everybody! For example, last Friday—just before we wanted to turn in—Mrs. Engineer Fried and Mrs. Liesel Fried dropped in on us. I had only heard about the latter while talking to the former; she claimed that you, dear Gusti, had played bridge with her on several occasions. She took a very long time before meeting me, even though she lives only five minutes away. Of course, she managed to arrive here in the middle of the worst mess due to my move. In addition, friend Engel also wanted to come over for a visit! But he ended up in the kitchen with me within five minutes because he did not care to socialize with the ladies!

He did bring me some very good puff paste; then he wanted to pontificate to me, but I dissuaded him from doing so. I think that made my life a lot easier in my own way!

On Friday morning I had to do some errands, so I ended up eating at the Engels after cooking for them the day before. *Krach Bum*. Things really didn't work for the first day because the amah didn't show up. She is always saying to me, "Mrs. Mayer, what would I do without you?" She is really grateful to me, but she just doesn't show it!

Now back again to Liesel Fried. Dear Gusti, she wants to send you her regards; she also asked for you to give her address to Lizzi Benedikt so she can get in touch with her. Obviously, she was extremely surprised that Eva had gotten married already. These ladies were also the bearers of some terribly sad news that really upset me. Can you imagine that Nellie Immergut, Hans Bleier's sister, died due to an accident? Walter Immergut, her husband, has probably visited you by now; I have already mentioned his name previously with my request to help him. I have spoken to Hans about the situation. He is of the opinion that we should advise him—as others have done—to wait until he arrives in Bogotá. Please tell him that, if you have the opportunity to talk to him. Most likely he heard about the accident already by sheer chance. The sequence of events happened as follows: After closing the store, Nellie was on the way home by pedicab.

Close to her apartment there is a busy intersection at Edinburgh road. There an MP jeep backed into Nellie's pedicab. Nellie was thrown out and fell on the back of her head and lost consciousness immediately. She was taken to the general hospital and died four hours later, without regaining consciousness. As usual here, her purse was stolen immediately so that nobody could identify her.

Poor Mrs. Bleier stayed up all night, as well as Nellie's son, Edi. Everybody suspected the worst; the worried people made unsuccessful phone calls all night long until Dr. Braun found her at the general hospital in the morning. I am writing all these details to you so that you can retell them to poor Walter Immergut, just as I have described that sad event. There was a memorial service for her at Kiochow Road, the same place where we had the service for your father; very many people attended. They played two chorales, followed by a close friend's talk, Dr. Weissberger, who spoke warmly on behalf of her friends; after all, she had been a very wonderful and helpful human being, no matter what the circumstances were. We, your father and I, really loved her; your father always had a splendid opinion of her. He used to say about her that she had the brains of a man. I think that I have written about her repeatedly. This tragedy deeply affected all of us who knew her personally. Obviously, I visited Mrs. Bleier during the early evening and plan to see her again tomorrow. I know that she really likes me, and I would be delighted to help her to survive this particularly tragic period. Poor Walter will have a very difficult time ahead of him, but now he needs to create a new future for himself. When I saw Nellie for the last time, I found her very upset at the thought that she had to send her husband away; so therefore she then became so much closer to me. "I just don't know if I am doing the right thing; up to now we have been lucky enough to keep our families together. So now there is a very big hole. Who knows when I will see my husband again!" She used to say, "You won't feel any pain if you don't hurt!" And now this tragedy! So now I have written all the details to you; you may use this information as you see fit.[99] Hans also told me that he has been invited

---

99   Käthe and Rudy Weiner told Walter Immergut about the death of his wife when he visited them in Oakland. Edi Immergut, the son of Nellie and Walter, was a teenager in Shanghai

to the American consulate to establish his claims resulting from this accident. The jeep driver was dismissed immediately. He wants to at least reach Hans so that he can help Edi to study in America. That was Nellie's heart's desire! Perhaps this utterly tragic accident will give him a chance for that study if dear Felix can help Walter in that quest. That's all I can say about that very tragic chapter. Nellie was exceptionally popular, just as she deserved.

Yesterday I received a very sweet letter from Elli, one from Paula Reiner, as well as the one from Lilli that you, dear Gusti, passed on to me; they seem to have been in the mail for almost one month.

I think that Lore has a particular talent for sewing; perhaps that would be a good career choice for her. I feel very badly what you, dear Gusti, write about Karl. But he isn't responsible for that. His nerves are just not in the very best shape; furthermore, the very difficult times have taken their toll on him. It would have been very good for him to get married. It's just not good to remain alone! It seems easier when there are two people together. I have been hearing that students encounter many extra difficulties in Czechoslovakia if they have not previously attended Czech-speaking schools.

For Wednesdays I have arranged a standing get-together since my friends want to visit me, but the telephone doesn't always work. I plan to go to the consulate to tell them about my new address; I also plan to ask if perhaps some new papers have arrived, as well as show the new numbers cited by you, dear Käthe. Most likely that won't really help, but it's worth a try. Obviously, dear Käthe, your description of San Francisco's zoo was of great interest to me. It would be just wonderful if I could have joined you for that zoo visit. I am very impatient, but regrettably nobody can do anything about that.

Apparently the papers for various other people seem to be in process, but generally the emigration process for the United States seems to be much slower than that for Australia. Next Saturday, Annemarie Pollack, a cousin of the Bleiers, is leaving for Bradford in England using the first English visa. I gave her Olga Deutsch's address; she

---

at the time of the accident. He also visited the Weiners in Oakland. He later earned a Ph.D. in the United States.

would love to know a person to whom she can turn for advice. She is very smart and has a Ph.D., but she is sort of impractical. Otherwise she is a very nice person. I don't know if Olga is the right advisor for her, but I know of nobody else.

Continued on 18 March

So now I have had my first bath after two and three quarters years—it was a sheer delight! What do you think of the fact that I truly enjoyed that bath? But we were very happy that at least we had a shower in Hongkew. At the moment, Mr. Strehlen is the co-owner of the best restaurant in Shanghai; as his first guest he wanted to offer me a recommendation for Mr. Jordan; he is supposedly very nice and may be able to help me a little bit. I am not going to visit the consulate until tomorrow because today our neighborhood was so badly flooded that you could not travel anywhere except by rickshaw. Schwarz was of the opinion that another day's delay would not hurt my situation; so I postponed my visit by one day. It's just unbelievable hereabouts when it rains hard. It has been raining here for several weeks, and the sewers cannot drain for lack of sufficient pitch. So therefore the water forms large and small lakes. There has been such a large lake in front of our house so that I could not go out yesterday without a rickshaw.

You probably have received my power of attorney; I'll keep on waiting for the Pilsen case[100] until I receive more details about it. Hannerl has already sent me some pictures of herself and her children. The past years didn't fail to leave their traces on her. That's just what happens to all of us! Gerhard called me and offered me his help for my move; but instead Schwarz helped me out. In the meantime I haven't paid him for his help. Most likely he won't accept any money, so I will have to find some other way of compensating him. They are definitely the opposite of being petty, but just as always so far, I don't like to receive gifts. I just feel very badly at day's beginning. I am in

---

100   Erna's family owned a large home in the center of Pilsen as well as a share in the Pilsener Urquel brewery. Both were confiscated by the Nazis.

good health as of now, but my day just seems to be too long! I still cannot take walks outside. But at least I hope to find some volunteer job. The day after tomorrow I plan to travel to Hongkew so that at least I can enjoy some more interesting distractions there. So now that's enough about me! That's just very boring stuff.

Continued on 19 March

I am writing in pieces; yesterday evening I just didn't get back to my letter after coming home from the Bleiers. First of all I found your letter, dear Glaubers, which had been forwarded from Pointroad. Secondly, I treated my landlords to a movie. So then I was quite busy reading to myself—and aloud to my friends. And thus I finally got to bed at 11:30. As always, I was overjoyed to read your letter; obviously, I laughed out loud about Beech-Nut Coffee![101] Picking that brand name for genuine coffee must have been a very creative idea! Lore is a very sweet girl; I am very proud that she considers me her confidant! If time permits I plan to write her separately. I am about to go to the consulate today to give them your information. In addition, by sheer coincidence I called the Engels while visiting with the Bleiers. He told me that a letter for me had arrived from you, my dear Weiners. So I plan to visit the Engels after the visit to the consulate and get ready to send this letter. All of you are so very nice to me. Yesterday I almost went crazy with the idea that perhaps I might have an early chance to join you. But please put your mind at ease about whether I can book an early ship's passage ticket. I'll just act like a spendthrift by flying to the United States. I am just yearning so very much. All of you seem to be so very busy—I am just amazed that you can manage all your affairs so well. I actually cannot remember Bulova, but I used to know his brother-in-law, Landsmann, very well. But never mind, I am already quite old and stupid. I am delighted to hear that Pauli Eckstein has been lucky to have already arrived over

---

101   When coffee was unavailable in Europe during the war years, beechnuts were ground for ersatz coffee.

there. Of course, it seems very sad that poor Elte didn't survive to make this trip.

With respect to things to take along: local silk products are neither well made nor cheap. Everything over here is insanely overpriced. Yesterday I studied the prices of canned coffee—one pound of coffee now costs eight thousand Shanghai dollars, and currently the Shanghai dollar is worth four U.S. dollars. Of course, I cannot demand that much for your coffee cans, but I always ask for the price of the best available coffee in the coffee store. But please don't send me any more since other people here also receive parcels; therefore there seems to be no big demand.

So now I just hope that this waiting will end very soon, and at that point I plan to give away a lot of my possessions. I have reached the conclusion that I should travel with only two pieces of hand luggage, but in that case I won't arrive as a rich mother and grandmother. But I will carry along lots of love, with the hope that I can still be a little bit helpful to somebody.

When you write your next letter, please be sure to include your warmest regards to the Schwarzes and the Eitelbergs! Otherwise I'll be unable to pass on your letter because these folks would feel very hurt—they always have been absolutely wonderful to me. She has never said an angry word to me personally, but sometimes her temper gets the better of her. Dear Weiners, Mr. Bleier is asking you to write to him directly so that he can read your letter personally; that would help him overcome his sister's recent death more easily. Usually a lot of people gather over here; recently I promised to visit him to mend his socks. That is not a condescending action, but I do him that favor very happily because they have always been very nice to me, and really appreciate my favors. I guess that I am only half-satisfied when I can do them a favor.

So now let me end this letter; I'll probably add some more while at the Engels' office. Please accept my kisses for each and every one of you, as well as for all the Blochs, the Rosensteins, and Mawei, to whom Mrs. Platschek sends many hearty greetings. *Nebbich*, she is very depressed that the Ecksteins are no longer alive. Of course, I cannot omit warmest regards to the Neubauers and to Fred. I keep on thinking of all of them, even though sometimes I may have forgotten to send greetings to them. So Kisses ...

[Handwritten addition]

Just came back from a visit to the consulate; there was nothing new for me, but I did notify them of my new address. So I'll have to keep on waiting until they call my number. There is nothing else for me to do. Dear Rudy, many thanks for your letter, which I plan to answer within a few days.

Many kisses,
Mother

[First page missing]

Page 2

My dear Gusti, you asked me which Czech bank handles my Pilsen account. To the best of my recollection, that bank was the Pilsner Bank. Since Hans Berger is still in Pilsen, somebody at the Pilsner Brewery may remember. I just don't have any relevant documents with me. When we were leaving, your father emptied his desk and the file cabinet, but did not take anything relevant with him. My bank account in Pilsen was seized by the Nazis to pay the taxes for the Leopold Mayer firm in Vienna.[102] You may be able to get some information from our firm's custodian, Treuhandsgesellschaft "Donau" VI, 56 Linke Wienzeile 4, Attention Herr Jiresch, who had been administering our firm. Under the prevailing circumstances he seems to act fairly decently. I still remember that I had to leave all the Pilsen-related documents there. So now I would like to know whose name should appear on the Power of Attorney. There is a Czech club here in Shanghai; Major Steppan here is an authorized secretary for the Czech consulate in Chungking. I am certain that I can complete this Czech power of attorney here without any problems. Probably it seems advisable to pursue our Kagran claims jointly with Elli and Fredi.[103] Dr. Hiller (office on Brandstaette in Vienna) was the lawyer who helped us retrieve the few things that we could take with us from Vienna. I plan to contact Margit Mayer, who also has signed a power of attorney. She had that document legalized at the U.S. consulate; I plan to do the same thing with my document. At the same time I plan to send notarized copies of father's death certificate.

You, Gucki, have asked me about my clothes, underwear, and shoes. I still have an ample supply of all these items. Thank God, I have had no accidents here, but I need to walk most of the day in sandals since my feet cannot stand any leather. My feet seem to be "offended" when they sense any leather! I think that my present shoes should last

---

102   <u>Leopold Mayer Bleiche, Farberei und Appretur</u> - bleaching and dyeing plant was owned and operated by Hans and Fritz Mayer before it was seized by the Nazis.

103   Fredi (Fritz) Mayer was Hans's brother and partner. Elli was his wife.

another three years; my feet have worsened with time, but my shoes did not change to conform to my feet. So I am still an *untam*[104] as far as my shoes are concerned. And as I get older, most likely my feet will get worse! But I'll see what happens. Perhaps I'll hear about an ingenious shoemaker who can make me a pair of shoes on a trial basis.

I don't know if the Duldners have left town. Apparently Karl D. received a job offer from Sweden, but could not get a ship's ticket; so the Swedish offer was withdrawn because they couldn't wait that long for him. Now he has an engagement here as of 1 January to build a local factory. But the client wants to wait for a few months with the hope that the prices here will decrease. He is already on salary, with the prospects for a partnership in the firm. So he can look forward to a nice future. Engineer Schwarz put him in touch with this firm. There are some very rich people here. Fritz has set his mind on returning to Vienna, but his wife refuses to join him there; she wants to stay in Shanghai with her younger son who is making an excellent living here. His wife claims that she just cannot share her life with her family's murderers. Except for a few people, nobody has moved away from here, with the exception of Professor Przibram, who received a job offer from Prague.

So now I think that I have answered all your questions. There is nothing new to report about me. I am healthy and keep gaining some weight. So please don't worry about me. Normally here you gain weight in the winter and lose it during the summer. But I hope not to be here by summertime. The Engels still want to stay here for a while, but their daughter has a sister in England, or would like to bring them to the United States. He seems to like to continue living here because the general hue and cry about moving away has stopped. Only the Germans are being urged to leave. If you are truly convinced that you want to stay here, you can always find some Chinese person to act as your guarantor, since they want to improve their personal income. Here you can fix almost every problem with money.

I hope that you, dear Kati, have benefited from your vacation, and that you are not working too much. Sigmund wrote to me that

---

104   Awkward person

all of you are overworked. I am just afraid that he is absolutely correct, but I cannot redirect you from here. I am firmly convinced that situation will no longer prevail when I am with you. So I just want to implore you to manage your strength a little better, even though the job may take a little longer. To my regret, I cannot relieve the men's workload.

Some time ago Mrs. Engler got stuck in Manila; has she arrived in good shape in the United States? Sad to say, her husband died just a few days before their planned departure from here. Earlier today Mrs. Glueckmann died unexpectedly after a short illness. Her husband is Miss Margulies's cousin; he used to be a big cheese for the Joint. If you don't know it already, Miss Margulies was the Joint's representative and organizer here until she was interned. She and Mr. Siegel were our guests in our Bubbling Well apartment; they were introduced to us by the Glueckmanns.

So that's enough schmoozing for us.

Many loving kisses to all of our beloved ones—big and little—from your Mother

Clara

Erna's sister, Clara Schoenmann stayed behind in Vienna after Erna and Hans left in November 1940. She wrote to them each week and they replied as often. She wrote about their fruitless efforts to emigrate to Portugal. She had to describe to Erna and Hans the unexpected death of her husband, Jacques, on January 23, 1941.

The Nazis required Jews remaining in Vienna to give up their large apartments and share housing in specified districts. Clara had to move in with friends after her husband's death. She reported on the deaths, illnesses and displacements of their many friends and relatives left in Vienna and passed on what little news she had about their sister Paula, who was still in Pilsen.

Clara's last letter was dated October 4, 1941. She was deported to Poland and then to a concentration camp on October 15, 1941.[105] Nothing more is known about Clara or Paula. Erna saved the letters from Clara. After the war she sent them to Clara's daughter, Hanna, who had settled in England.

From Erna to Hanna Schoenmann Oppenheimer
23 March 1946

My dear ones all,

Recently I wrote to you, dear Hanna, and promised to send all the correspondence from your dear parents. So now it is your mother's birthday and I re-read all these letters once more before sending them to you. This is a greeting from the other part of the world. So very much has turned out to be very different from what we had expected. But all of that came to naught as we were wracking our minds.

Ten days ago Mr. Schwarz, Mrs. Eitelberg, and I moved to the French area. Naturally these accommodations are much nicer than

---

105   Record of deportation appears in the Documentation Archive of the Austrian Resistance Movement. www.doew.at

in Hongkew. But I have absolutely nothing to do which has really gotten on my nerves. I was longing for an invitation to the Consulate, but nothing is stirring, even though the children wrote me that I have all the necessary approvals. I have had it with waiting around. There is nothing much to report from here. Right now we are in the bad rainy season; there is a big enough lake in front of our house that you need a rickshaw to leave the house. I am living very near to the Hahns and plan to visit them very soon. Thank God, I hear from the children on a very regular basis—these letters are rays of sunshine for me.

I would like to stop here; otherwise I would be complaining to you, but you cannot do anything about the situation here. I hope that you are doing well in all aspects of life, and that I will receive some news from you very soon – your letters are also rays of sunshine for me. I get really attached to each one of them.

So my heartiest kisses and greetings your ever-loving

Aunt Erna

17 April 1946

My dear Rosensteins,

I was overjoyed with your dear letter dated 26 March. So I want to respond immediately, even though not much is new here. Besides, you keep on top of our doings through our children. In general, very little happens, which is just fine with me. You know about all the tragic and sad events. Obviously, all of us have been deeply touched by them, particularly since they have been very much on our minds for the past three years. But that's life, to our regret! It seems so very sad that we have managed to survive all our hardships, but when things are about to get better, we find that so many people are no longer alive. I have just been wondering why so far I haven't heard anything from your parents. It seems perfectly OK how you have managed things, but I am still of the opinion that older people can survive change better than the younger ones. I am very sorry to hear that you are unhappy with Oskar's situation. I guess that he should have gotten married some time ago. Actually it is not too late for him. But nobody can talk him into getting married; he just has to make up his own mind as to what he really wants to do. How is Otto[106] doing? I just hope that he is doing well. Dear Truderl, my hair has become grayer and thinned out—that's why I didn't want to be photographed—and my figure has changed. In addition, I try to keep my hair tied together more closely. Everybody tells me that I look quite well, nor do I have any reason to complain about my health, thank God. My accommodations are really fine; the Kollmanns have also moved into a better apartment. On the other hand, the commode is less than satisfactory. So they still don't know what they are going to do about that. Recently we got a short letter from Fritzi who is trying to convince them to move to New Zealand. But over there Egon could not continue his medical practice; and I am convinced that he has no talent for becoming a businessman. By the way, tomorrow

---

106   Oskar and Otto Bloch were Trude Rosenstein's brothers. Oskar settled in Argentina, married there. Otto went to Palestine.

I will give them this letter, and then they will write their own letter to you. It is pretty bad for the Jewish refugees in Shanghai. People who emigrated elsewhere have acquired local citizenship by now and settled down. But we here will have to start all that again.[107] All these years as refugees have left their mark on all of us. I am very happy that you get together with the Weiners and our other loved ones so frequently, and that you are satisfied with your new careers. I also got a letter from the "Moderns;" how did they manage to establish independent careers? After all, that's quite an achievement at their ages where they have finally settled into a comfortable life. In any case, it seems quite nice that they were able to reorient their careers. I am assuming that you, dear Ernst, are not thinking of moving back to Kuffners in Vienna, even though that offer may be very tempting. The whole idea of moving back to Vienna seems to be just completely odious to us. Now that's enough schmoozing! We hope that you continue to do well, and I want to convince myself personally that this is the truth!

Warmest regards to your parents and your siblings.
And now feel kissed by your Aunt Erna

---

107   It was still difficult to get entry visas to the United States, Australia and Palestine after the war ended in 1945. Many refugees waited in Shanghai and in Hongkew for sponsors and quota numbers to come up. Most had left by 1949.

22 April 1946
All my dear beloved ones,

There is actually nothing new to report since I will not get any mail this week, probably due to the Easter holiday. But I am starting this letter with the hope that some mail will arrive tomorrow. In addition, on Saturday I received the notice that another packet has arrived. I plan to pick it up on Wednesday. So I still don't know whom to thank since the notice didn't list the sender. I don't want to repeat myself as always, since that doesn't help anyone. But please stop sending these packages; more than likely they won't reach me because they take at least two months to get here. The most recent package was still addressed to Pointroad and was then forwarded to me. And people usually say that the Chinese mail doesn't work well.

For the time being there seems to be no progress at the U.S. consulate. I was there on 16 April; an official told me that the police report [108] still had not arrived. Therefore I'll go there again later this week. UNRRA helped me get the Chinese exit visa that has already been stamped into my passport; now I just need the American immigration visa. Finally a U.S. consul general has been here for the past few days; reportedly things are supposed to start moving faster now. I can only hope, let that be true with God's help! It is Easter Monday today so that all of you may have an extra day off—your daily work probably is a big strain for all of you. To my regret, here every day is a holiday!

On Saturday the Engels moved to another apartment. So I wanted to help them settle in. But some workmen were still there, in addition to the amah. Mrs. Engel was dead tired, so I said good-bye and headed back to Hongkew. Mrs. Engel started worrying where I would eat lunch; I told her not to worry. I went to the former Japanese food market, where you used to be able to find the best bargains. But since the departure of the Japanese there are very few customers. I picked up a nice cutlet there and then went home.

---

108   Certifying that no adverse information exists in the police records.

First I stopped in with the Kriegls, who live closest to me on my way home. The fare on the electric streetcar has tripled since yesterday. That was their Easter present! But it took only twenty minutes of walking time from the Engels, and that's no real problem for me. Of course, the Kriegls were extremely pleased with the honor of my visit. Obviously, they refused to let me eat my cutlet, but invited me to be their surprise guest. Mrs. Kriegl finally got some news from her sister and Liese Sedlarik, in Vienna, to whom you, dear Gusti, had sent the food packages.

The Kriegls were deeply touched that you, dear Gusti, even wrote separately to Sedlarik that you had sent two food packages. I was extremely proud of my very good daughter! Her father had died in August 1945; her mother was very sick and in the hospital. So now here's a *pferdefuss*[109] for you, dear Gusti: can you please send another food package? Please send it directly to Mrs. Kriegl's sister, who is still in her old apartment—a fact that Mrs. Kriegl was unaware of. I wanted her to wait to send the next package until at least one of the earlier ones has been acknowledged. But Mrs. Kriegl insists adamantly that the Viennese are starving and that her conscience dictates that she needs to do everything possible for her relatives. Apparently Mr. Kriegl has sent some money to Vienna, but I am of the opinion that the food items are worth their weight in gold. So here is the list of desired foods: 1 lb of corn meal, 2 lbs of butter or shortening, 1 lb of cheese, 1 lb of dried or canned milk, 1 lb of sugar, 1 lb of jam, 1 lb of coffee, and 1 lb of chocolate. The address is: Mr. Josef Gozdal, Vienna 21/141, Freytaggasse 14/32/2/11. It should be obvious that you should shop for these items however you can make it easy for yourself. You are welcome to make any substitutions, as you feel necessary. The Kriegls do not really care if your choices are more expensive. They are just extremely happy for your help. I just hope that this request will not overload you, dear Gusti.

So now here is request number two: Mrs. Dr. Eitelberg would like to ask you, dear Gusti, to get in touch with her cousin, Mrs. Gertrude Parker, to remit thirty dollars to her. The reason seems to be that Mrs.

---

109   Literally, "horse's leg" - a particularly nervy request.

Dr. Eitelberg had ordered several items from Mrs. Parker, who did not want to be paid for them; but Mrs. Eitelberg just doesn't want her not to be repaid. Mrs. Eitelberg is of the opinion that you can call her to convince her that the shipped items have been most welcome, but that they would feel better about the reimbursement, which would not really hurt them. As soon as you can write me about carrying out this transaction, they will give me the equivalent amount here. Here is Mrs. Parker's address: 200 Pinehurst Avenue, New York City 33. Mrs. Parker used to work for Penizek & Reiner, but now runs her own business and has a telephone.

So now you have more than enough errands for one day. I hope that the expenses will not break you. I really don't need the money here, but when somebody else asks me for an occasional favor, I just cannot say no. And of course, I hope that you, my dear Käthe, won't be jealous of Gusti because of the two errands; but I believe that you are much busier than Gusti, and that sending the packages from New York will be simpler.

After eating so very well at the Kriegls, I continued to walk further into inner Hongkew and stopped in to see Mrs. Deutschberger; her emigration plans seem to be at the same stage as mine. After schmoozing with her for a little while I went to the Duldners, where coffee time is always the very best. After schmoozing there for about two hours I walked to the Kollmanns, but they were not home. Then I stopped in with the Posamentiers and then took the electric streetcar. On the streetcar I met Margit Weiner,[110] who joined me in traveling home since we live near one another. This afternoon I am planning to visit them in order to insert another piece of material into their comforter. Dear Käthe, now I am just practicing for working in your household!

With the help of some acquaintances, the Kollmanns found a beautiful apartment in Shanghai's former English quarter without paying any "key money,"[111] but they had to pay for refurbishing the place at substantial expense. Furthermore, they are shaking about the

110   Margit Weiner is not related to the Rudolph Weiner family. None of the Weiners or Stein-Weiners in Shanghai are related.
111   A bribe usually paid to the landlord for transferring the lease.

possibility that they may be expelled from this apartment. Regrettably, there is a major apartment shortage in Hongkew, particularly for modern ones; the situation seems to be even worse for Chinese residents. For example, at the beginning of last week a large group of Chinese came into Sacra Lane and demanded that the refugees should move out so that they could reoccupy the apartments that they had to abandon under pressure from the Japanese. Luckily, the Joint and UNRRA did intervene on the refugees' behalf, but nobody knows if quiet can be restored. On Friday the same protests were repeated in the Waysideheim. On Monday the Chinese threatened to return with one thousand men to force the evacuation of that home. These are some of our miserable problems. Earlier this week I had the opportunity to talk to Herr von Stoery He also told me that there was a major problem with the Jewish refugees in Shanghai. The Chinese usually reject us completely and only respect those strangers who are big spenders. So therefore the Chinese do not care at all about the poor Jewish refugees here. As we usually observe, "It's very hard to be a Jew!" I got a letter from Hannah that I have already answered. In the meantime Walter Immergut moved to another country again, according to last week's telegram from him. He's a very poor soul!

Continued on 23 April:

Finally I visited the Stein-Weiners. When I came home, there was Gerhard to bring me a package. He said that he also had received a letter, but didn't have it with him. He promised to deliver it to Mr. Schwarz's office on Tuesday. Mr. Schwarz did go to his office that day, but did not get the letter because Gerhard had not brought it by that time. Kitty Teltscher will remind Gerhard again so that I can get the letter, I hope.

Dear Gusti, the cotton outfit is absolutely beautiful. Also many thanks for all the other items; it just seems impossible for me to eat everything you sent. I need to tell you that I have to have my clothing altered daily for a larger size. I was also at the post office. I got my stuff very quickly because today is a Jewish holiday; I was finished in twenty minutes. As I do every Tuesday, I took the streetcar to visit Mother Bleier, where I can always find something that needs sewing. I hope that you have sent no more packages. But in the interest of other package recipients, let me offer the following few ground rules: puddings always seem to arrive with torn wrappers; frequently half of it is missing in the package. Furthermore, the soup cubes and the chocolate bits had been combined and were open. At the time I could only think of a combination of chocolate and garlic! But actually that sounds like a good combination. Both items are very good, but not as a combination. Gusti, you really think of everything! I could have really used the rubber insoles that you sent, but they were unfortunately far too small. I am going to check with a shoe repair store if he wants to buy them. I will also check if the tailor would like to buy the thread. I plan to try to sell one half of the cotton to Mrs. Eitelberg. I think that I can get about three to four dollars per yard—I hope that you didn't pay much more. I am not a good salesperson and my customers like to pay only very little for my merchandise. I hope that you have already received my letter saying that I have received my letter from the consulate—so please stop sending packages to me! I have caused you a lot of expense, in addition to sending the food parcels on behalf of my friends. As a precautionary measure I would recommend adding a layer of newspaper to items like chocolate and puddings. Their boxes have corners that tend to puncture the paper bags. But as I said earlier, I am offering this advice only on behalf of others. Earlier today I received my shots; I still have to go back for some more shots.

Tomorrow, or on the day after tomorrow, I plan to visit the UNRRA office; perhaps they can tell me how I can proceed faster. I have heard the rumor that a ship is supposed to leave in about six to eight weeks that is supposed to accommodate all emigrants with visas based on a "preferred quota" slot. So I am just full of hope. Today I got a letter from the Blochs dated 8 March. Please send them my warmest regards and I will write to them directly very soon. The hot summer arrived as of Easter Sunday. My print dresses are just too heavy for this heat; as of tomorrow I plan to wear cotton outfits. Today I went to the Russian temple, which is very huge and beautiful. But they had a miserable cantor, as well as someone well learned from a yeshiva who rattled on in Yiddish, so I couldn't understand a word. That is supposed to be the religious service for our Jewish refugees but it is much more orthodox than we are used to. The Russians don't pay much attention to the prayers; they keep talking to one another instead. So you can understand from my letter that one such temple visit was enough.

I am very sorry that your letters have not arrived yet. It seems so much easier when I can answer questions posed in your letters.

So all of you—adults and children—stay well and feel kissed frequently by your Mother

5 May 1946

From Erna

c/o Schwarz, Defris & Co

11968 Jinkeeroad   Room 23

All my dear ones,

I want to confirm receiving your letters, my dear Weiners, dated 12
April and 18 April , as well as Walter Immergut's letter; I want you
to thank Walter in the meanwhile and then discuss his letter. I also
got the letter from the dear Glaubers dated 16April. I have been a
little nervous since I normally count on getting a weekly letter from
you on time, but then this time there was a delay so that both letters arrived on the same day. After all, I have been really spoiled.
So I started worrying wrongly that you, dear Käthe, just had gotten
so overloaded that you ran out of time to write to me. Dear Käthe,
please be smart enough to learn that you cannot conquer time like
"fighting City Hall;" sometimes things take longer than expected. It
was very nice of you, dear Rudy, to relieve Käthe of her writing chore
at that time. You wrote so many details and very clearly so that I really feel well informed. That's very nice of you.

I am terribly sorry to hear that poor Walter created so much ex-
citement. On the other hand you are probably very glad that you
were so very helpful to him. So that experience must have been very
tragic for you. I am going to see Mother Bleier tomorrow – or at the
latest on the day after tomorrow – to discuss this entire matter with
her. According to my best knowledge, she would prefer to emigrate
to Bogota since she sees a better life for herself, as well as earning a
living more easily than in the USA. She also told me that running a
household is "not her cup of tea;" she would prefer knitting scarves
(or something like that) – it is very difficult to offer advice to someone, especially when you don't know the country or its people. Furthermore, that's too much of a responsibility for me. But I'll talk to
her in any case.

Yesterday I went to the UNRRA office for the second time, as well as to the Consulate with Captain Wells' letter. There they assured me that all the papers in my file are in good shape, and that I should no longer worry. The police report is now here and that they have requested a "call number" for me in San Francisco. This number is needed to let me land in the USA. But I need to restrain my enthusiasm temporarily because this process will take at least until the end of June. Please "cross your fingers" that everything will proceed as promised. This reminds me of an era long ago when you were treated nicely by a government official. But the Consulate operates as if it were a very busy retail store – everything tends to move slowly! But I am quite content with the assurance that all my paper work now is OK.

In addition to this event Mr. Schwarz observed his birthday on 1 May that was duly celebrated. I donated a Linzertorte and homemade chocolate cubes because he loves to *nosh*. He received some nice presents there. In the evening the Duldners came for a visit. By that I mean that Lusia and Helen came, each of them with a son. Fritz needed to stay home to guard their place – here nobody dares to leave the home unguarded. Just so you can see how well we eat, here is the menu. Obviously I also attended, but normally I refuse all such invitations when guests are invited; but this time I just could not say NO. There were stuffed eggs in the French style, salad with mayonnaise, pork roast with green peas, rice, cucumber salad, whip cream with fruit salad, and black coffee. All these dishes appeared in huge quantities. There were also some tortes, but nobody could manage to eat them anymore. As I have been writing you, everything needed is available here; this was true even during war time.

Last Thursday I picked up another food parcel from you, dear Emil, at the Customs Office. I was very smart to arrange my errands by going first to the Customs to submit my claim check, then to the UNRRA Office, and then back to Customs for the package. So I spent only one hour on these three errands. In the meantime it became noon, so I went to the Engels who live near that area to eat lunch with them. They now have a Chinese "cook boy" to serve all of us a delicious Chinese Chow meal. Then I rested for the walk through Hongkew. I chose an alternate route that took me over an hour instead of the usual twenty minutes. I was very happy to be in the Ghetto again. You cannot imagine how the local streets twist and turn so that you can get totally disoriented. But this new route gave me the advantage to pass the Chaufongheim on the way. That's where the old Schwarz couple lives; therefore I dropped in on them as I had planned to do for some time. So thus I made another stop on my "social route." Along the way I also did some shopping and then stopped in at the Posamentiers to give them some newspapers. But they told me happily that Walter had given them a subscription and so they would no longer need my newspapers. They are also very happy with Walter's offer to send them affidavits. They would like to go to USA if they can leave earlier. P. just isn't young anymore, and Shanghai has taken its toll on him. I'd like to tell D. as soon as feasible about this possibility as you, dear Emil, write that the Schwarzes and the Engels really would like to stay here. The former is trying hard to get an Australian permit while the Engels would like to move to the USA. It certainly seems easy to earn a living here, but the Chinese are not kindly disposed toward our refugees. Nobody can predict how this could change some day in the future. Mr. Schwarz and Mr. Engel seem to earn a pretty good living, but they are also big spenders; therefore it seems that they cannot save very much. Mr. Schwarz has also spent a great deal of money on their apartment; he is counting on getting all of his investment back quite readily. If he has time enough to liquidate his apartment, then he may be right. But sometimes you receive your travel permits unexpectedly with the need to prepare for your almost immediate departure. Yesterday I read that Oskar Hoffmann is saying goodbye to his friends in the newspaper. He left to join his daughter in Australia. So the departure pattern of our refugees has been gradual and steady. But that's very good since people are gradually reaching their desired goal.

Yesterday I just didn't know what to do with myself so I went to a movie. It didn't leave any lasting impression; if you skip this movie, you haven't missed much. But sometimes I feel an urgent need to break up my day. This week I bought a pair of brown summer shoes — a type of sandals – that will enable me to wear my insoles. Since I can walk well in these shoes, I ordered another pair in black. The converted price is about $15; I do find this price quite high, but to my regret I cannot wear ready-made shoes. Somehow I believe that such shoes would be even more expensive over there.

Dear Gusti, the cotton dress is being altered right now; I sold the other one and plan to buy one with the proceeds. Right now, cotton dresses are very popular here, but their appeal keeps shrinking. Dear Käthe, I have sold the little dress you sent me and hope that you agree with my decision. Normally I sell some of the food since I cannot use up all of these items. And I also hope that I won't be here long enough to use up the rest.

In any case, I have been cooking "American Style." For example, for yesterday's lunch I had baked franks and noodle soup. Today I am having liver with rice and noodle soup again. I can buy the same noodle soups for 30 Shanghai cents each. Does that correspond to the price over there?

You really seem to have very many guests! I think that you are truly surpassing the numbers in Kagran! Dear Rudy, you are quite correct that these many guests were no real challenge since I had Julie[112] for cooking! Talking about Julie: so far I have had no news about her; can you get me her current address? My letters to the Lippas and to Emil T. seemed to have crossed with theirs. I wrote to them and they wrote to me; so all three of us are now waiting for a letter so that one of us can restart this correspondence.

I rarely see Hans Klinge, but he has told me that he is planning to start some sort of exporting business with Paul. In my humble opinion he lacks persistence and furthermore he just isn't a businessman. He has really needed a wife all along. As of now I am going to try to only answer letters. Dear Gusti, you have already written me about Trude. So now I hope that you will make an end very soon. It is a well-known saying that "You can't dance at two weddings at the same time!" As of now, things should be much better because Betty

---

112   Erna's cook in Kagran

has arrived in the United States. Please thank her for her note; I really look forward to see her in person again. I would like to thank Trude for her gift of chocolate candy. How do I rate so much loving attention? But the candy is really delicious! All of us here have become very spoiled by good food! And since all of us are *noshers*, we all have gained a lot of weight! Dear Gusti, Mrs. Dr. Eitelberg really enjoyed your note. Not one of her dresses fits her now without some major alterations!

Dear Gusti, are you making progress in your driver education program? Are there any prospects for your buying a car? Just please be cautious, but I don't want to preach! Are you, dear Emil, also learning to drive? You had already started to do that in Vienna, but you couldn't pursue that for lack of time. It's very nice to hear that Hans Adler is showing some interest in our situation. It seems utterly incredible that we might get back some of our things;[113] but I wouldn't be annoyed if that happened because that would make your lives easier. It is also a shame that Moidl[114] with her child has not yet come over. So it appears there is also some red tape over there. But actually the situation should be improving over there. The newspapers and periodicals have started to arrive here sequentially. So please stop my subscription to the Aufbau since my landlady is already an Aufbau subscriber who makes it available to me.

Mrs. Kriegl had you address the food parcel to Mrs. Sedlarik in Vienna because her mother is in the hospital right now. But she has already had a letter that her mother is back home; so you can send her the next parcel directly. She even deigned to send you a note directly to give you some satisfaction. I have always been amused by the fact that they have kept writing letters recently. They seem to be nice people, but sort of primitive! He was the one who sent the stamps. I'm delighted to hear that you are still keeping in touch with the Jabloners as long ago. Here his cousin runs a small, but fancy restaurant with the Strehlens; they seem to be doing very well. Alice is

---

113   Refers to Hans Adler's efforts to claim restitution for the home, possessions and factory in Kagran that were taken by the Nazis. Some restitution was received by Erna's daughters in 2006.

114   Hans Adler's wife

very lonely here because none of her family is here. The presence of any family members here would have made her life much easier.

I want to thank you very much for your offer of money. There is absolutely no reason to send me money. Obviously I'd rather have some money over there. I still have about $350; then I plan to sell my suitcase and my typewriter. I hope to get about $80 for both so that I should be able to get along on my own money here. If not, then the Engels and also the Hubers will give me any additional money needed. My spending has really increased dramatically due to the local monetary inflation. Dr. Janstein was lucky enough to "fall on the butter side." Are you in touch with him at all? He just didn't treat us nicely; now I am still very sorry that we gave him such a nice farewell present, a tie tack.

Herr Aubauer must have been an "arch Nazi" because he was never drafted into he Nazi army; he probably found a safe spot somewhere. Nobody needs to shed a tear for him! I am very sorry that Karl still has some mental problems. There's just nobody who knows how to treat that problem. Perhaps he will improve if he can find himself a job somewhere. Regretfully, one can get sicker much faster than cured!

So now let me turn to the Weiners because, by God, they are not my stepchildren! Dear Rudy, from your letter I understand that you caught another cold; I hope that it wasn't too serious and didn't last very long. I am really very impressed by your menus! Do you make *Windbeutel*[115] or can you buy them ready-made? I plan to stand there to watch you make them, just like a "country yokel." But I also know that I can learn to prepare all the convenience foods very quickly!

When you, dear Rudy, talk about Henry as able to spend money easily, perhaps you shouldn't consider that as a real problem. The main thing is that he will be able to earn the necessary money. Actually I am of the opinion that you should not be too modest to avoid satisfying your more expensive needs; that attitude will compel you to aim at earning some more money! Your letter also describes Lieserl as a *scrob* who has to rely on only her pocket money, presumably that

---

115   Cream puffs

won't be very much! Does Henry still sell newspapers? How come that he is allowed to do that, but George isn't? Aren't there any uniform legal regulations? Dear Rudy, you are really impressing me with your talent for carpentry! I seem to remember that the late Emperor Francis Joseph I was also an amateur carpenter. I can just imagine how proud you feel when you have completed a carpentry project. But now I am just waiting to hear that your better half may abuse you after discovering that special talent! So by the time I come, every bit of glue will have dried so I won't get stuck as happened so often in Kagran.

My dear ones!

This postscript was unintended. Just as I was finishing this letter, Gerhard arrived with your dear letter dated 26 March; it took a lot longer to arrive because it was so heavy. I just cannot tell you how happy I was to learn that he was leaving next Tuesday; he is planning to visit you, dear Rudy, or call you. I deeply applaud his well-deserved chance to finally return home to Gerti. He has done "yeoman service" for his extended family. So now you will have an excellent reporter who can explain the reason for my delay here and why my emigration plans are moving so slowly for me. But "never mind," now I am just laughing at the slow pace! I'd like to congratulate you on your new refrigerator; it must be a real blessing for you! We also have an icebox here in Honkew; but during our last year here we never bought any ice because nobody wanted to deliver it to our home; and it was too much to *schlep* it home. But only when it became nearly unbearably hot in our apartment did I go to the Schwarzes to cool off where I could get cold water since they had converted their refrigerator to oil. So enjoy your refrigerator in good health; I would like to join you to also enjoy it! Thank God, Mawei seems to be unbelievably capable because she can take care of herself without any help. I need to express my deepest respect for her! And, Katinka, you seem to be able to darn which just leaves me speechless. The main thing is that your home's laundry is done regularly. As you know, I visit people to do their darning jobs. But perhaps now you can save some of your darning for me.

I am very sorry that Loewy has died, but he was very lucky to reach his goal by joining his children and grandchildren. This was an act of God's mercy that – to our regret – your father just was not privileged to share. So I want to end here to write a separate note to my grandchildren.

Many and loving kisses from your
Mother

note written in English

My dear Helen and Henry:

I got today through uncle Karplus the nice picture what you made and mother send to me. I was surprised that you make it so nice and I find you are talented for painting. So I will keep it and they are hanging in my room. Now I think I have opportunity to see you soon. In short time you both will have birthdays and this will be nice if I can sing with the parents "happy birthday to you." What have you for wishes? Write me about this may be I may something buy here for you. So enough for to day you must laugh about my bad writing. I send you many kisses stay healthy and learn wider good in the school.

Your Grandmother

25 May 1946

All my loved ones,

First of all I want to confirm that I have received your letter dated 6 May from dear Emil, as well as the one from you, dear Rudy, dated 9 May. So I can only tell you the same thing. These letters are the sunshine in my life since the unending wait only leads to despair and has worn out my nerves. You are very correct in writing me that you are also very impatient. At my end, I find myself with another consular office problem that is causing yet another delay. I am certain that Gerhard has also explained it to you. Yesterday Mr. Fuchs went to the U.S. consulate again, this time without me. Apparently it makes no difference whether I am standing there or not. Usually, the consular official pulls out my file and then explains what the latest problem is. So the last word was that my file was OK, and they had sent a cable to Washington to get my call number. Perhaps someone can check in Washington to expedite my case—you should do that in any case. But I think that, hopefully, this call number will arrive here before this letter reaches you. I had my interview at the consulate at the same time as Mrs. Stein, and she got her visa yesterday.

Here is a counterexample for my case: Mrs. Deutschberger and her parents-in-law were the first Jewish refugees to receive their medical examinations at the consulate. Mr. Spitzer has had his visa for some time and left this week by ship, but Mrs. Deutschberger is still waiting here. Mrs. Bleier is supposed to visit me today; if she doesn't show up, I plan to take a streetcar to Hongkew to visit Mrs. Deutschberger to find out what is going on. Tomorrow I plan to visit the Stein-Weiners to get more details. By now I have lost all my desire to sit back and wait for things to happen; I am well aware of your plans, dear Käthe, so that I will be able to take a lot of your load off your shoulders. Of course, I would have to ask many questions. Dear Käthe, did you take over an existing enterprise, or will you have to acquire all the necessary equipment by yourself?[116] Just as dear Emil

---

116   Käthe established a private massage studio in Oakland. Rudy continued to work in the linen supply business.

and I had figured it out, we imagined that you, my dear Weiners, would establish a joint enterprise. If you didn't do so, you must have had very sound reasons for not doing that. I should think you would want to have the ability to represent one another, and I imagine a joint enterprise would make it easier for you to take time off.

Now I would like to describe the local situation to a small extent, since you, dear Rudy, wrote that Käthe has to drive eighteen miles to see one of her lady patients, and then receives only $5 for this treatment session. Nobody here would do that, except for a physician. For example, a hairdresser in Hongkew will charge only $5 for a single shampoo, and not even in a very nice beauty parlor. Of course, the better class of people does spend a lot more money. Therefore I tend to complain that I need to live on a certain amount of money; on the other hand, Mr. Schwarz says that the household expenses have jumped a lot, even though he spends his money quite readily. Currently I spend $50 per month for the food, for the boy, and for the small necessities, but excluding my rent. We used to spend about the same amounts while your dear father was still alive. And actually we lived better at that time than I do now, when I refuse to spend money on anything except for the necessities. For example, a streetcar round trip to Hongkew costs 25 cents—that sounds expensive enough from an American point of view![117] And there have been almost daily strikes to thwart that service! Last week there were no streetcars for five days. Similarly, nobody collected our garbage because the workers went on strike, just another strike in a series of strikes by the municipal workers.

Another example: one pound of rice now costs 43 cents and serves as the local standard. Dear Gusti, I was able to sell the cotton for $2.50 per yard, but I could not always get that price because cotton became readily available at a more reasonable cost. I hope that at this time I haven't sold it too cheaply. Thread is the only thing I have bought recently, but I needed it to mend my clothes. This year

---

117   In 1946 one nickel (five cents) would buy you a single ride on the New York City subway, or let you make a local phone call.

we did have wonderful cool weather, except for two very hot days, as well as a lot of rain. But today may get very hot.

With my thanks I would like to confirm the arrival of a letter from my dear Blochs; since I already wrote to them directly, I'll wait for their next letter before replying because I have nothing special to tell them. I am very sorry that you, dear Gustav, are having so much trouble with your eyes. I had already suspected something of that sort because your handwriting—particularly when in ink—had changed so radically. If someone like me has nothing to do all day long, you tend to start thinking a lot. It seems to be the worst when you have absolutely nothing to do because every day just seems endless. There is so much going on with you! Dear Gusti, please excuse Mrs. Eitelberg for taking so much of your time. I hope that you haven't sent anything recently to Gerhard's address. In any case he has asked Kitti Teltscher to forward my stuff, which seems to work well. Just let Mrs. Parker be responsible for sending things. Then you won't have to send things anymore—after all, she does own a business and has some staff people to whom she can delegate this task. So please don't let her take advantage of you! It certainly seems enough for you to send food parcels to the relatives of my various friends!

But the world has really shrunk when you, dear Gusti, hear from everybody that I am about to come. Yesterday I visited the Sachses, who want to send warmest regards to Paula Reiner. Please do the same for me; I was extremely sorry for her when I heard that she broke her hand. I hope that it has healed well by now so she is back to using it normally. One can only say that anything you don't have to suffer is sheer profit.

I told Mrs. Sachs that our *schmoozes* would continue until her departure for America. Around here everybody is a gossip! By the way, Mrs. Schaffir is Mrs. Eitelberg's friend, and according to her she is a good friend of Mrs. Eitelberg's sister, Mrs. Koditschek. The world has become very small! You, dear Emil, told us of some news: I am delighted that Elli just received her visa, but now has to wait for a berth on a ship. *Nebbich*, that's just the usual constraint! If you have one of the two necessary components, you need to really chase the other one. So now I hope that Karl can come very soon when he gets his visa. The big news is that Edith Steiner-Malz already had gotten this information from Gerhard. Hopefully, everything will fall into place—after all, she already has had many troubles along the way to emigration. I am also delighted to hear the good news about Rolly Geiringer. I hope that she is doing well physically and financially. I always see it as a good omen when people have a baby under these circumstances. Of course, even though more than enough children are born here, it is generally untrue that the people here are doing very well.

Last week the Klebanoffs, rich Russian Jews, as well as another refugee couple, were to fly to the United States. Their money for their seats was returned to them one hour before the departure time. Since their seats were needed for the military, the civilians had to stay back. That's just one example of the local situation. But I will try to manage my own case. Nothing can happen before I am summoned to the consulate. I have already booked a ship's ticket for December, but I plan to take advantage of any chance to travel. And I hope that somewhere there'll be a little spot for me!

Earlier this week I visited the Duldners, who send you their warmest regards; they also want to thank you for your empathy. Their relatives and friends want to send them affidavits since they will be unable to stay here, nor want to do so.

As of now, the Kollmanns have not made up their minds since that seems superfluous because you cannot start an emigration plan right now. Recently I wrote to Juli and Hohenberg. With that I think that I have answered all your questions for you, dear Emil. So now it is Rudy's turn.

In considering the rapid pace of your lives over there, I suspect that you may have too little time to read my long letters. I was very sorry to hear about the accident during your vacation trip where you had to return early; but you can thank the good Lord that everything still worked out. I assume that you, dear Rudy, had an open wound on your leg that somehow got infected. I am sure that you all needed that vacation quite badly. I hope that you will be able to make up for this disrupted trip and do it some other time when I am there to take care of the house and the children. Wish it were so already, *Allewei!*

I can imagine the surprise with Fred Markus.[118] I have been keeping an eye out for him, with the hope that I would run into him accidentally. But since he is now over there, I cannot foresee an opportunity to see him.

By the way, I saw Edith Eichberg, who occasionally has been asking about all the Markuses. She keeps partially informed through a common friend. Penicillin is used very frequently here, but it is hard to find; sometimes it proves very helpful to get it from the army. Thank God for the existence of such a wonder drug! Unfortunately, it didn't help Mr. Duldner, but perhaps the physicians did not know how to use it properly.

Tomorrow is Mrs. Dr. Eitelberg's birthday, but we don't plan to celebrate because she is in such a bad mood right now. Through Mrs. Parker she found out that her ex-husband died in Malzgasse[119] at age forty-two. She doesn't know what has happened to her son, who was living with her ex-husband and supposedly was present at his death. So nobody really knows. At the same time there was a letter from Mr. Engineer Schwarz's wife; she had enclosed a picture of herself and their son, and also asked him what their future would be. Obviously, this has made a nervous wreck out of her. But please don't mention any of this! Schwarz is determined not to abandon them. On the other hand, he feels very sorry about his wife and son. Apparently, this couple has always postponed any discussion of their future, where other couples normally always have discussed this topic.

Otherwise, nothing of any importance is happening that would interest you. Right now, your child is learning to play the trumpet. I am already getting used to that since there is a Chinese school next door where they practice their music very diligently.

Here is something I have always wanted to ask you: do ladies wear hats over there? Here we are comfortable without any hat in the summer and winter. Of course, I can have a hat fixed for myself.

118   Rudy's nephew. After emigrating from Vienna he finished high school in Chicago and served in the United States Navy.
119   A transit camp

I am not planning to buy anything new. But in any case I will need something during the trip.

Margit Weiner just came in to complain that I have not visited her for a week. She wants to send you her warmest regards; she was very happy to hear that Grete Fuert is so concerned for her mother. She would like to tell her that she would write her directly, but doesn't know where Mrs. Fuert lives.

The address for the Stein-Weiners is Avenue Joffre 1920, Flat 700.

Just now I am returning from Hongkew, where I visited Mrs. Deutschberger. Apparently, her case seems to be on hold; she is still waiting for the phone call that her call number has arrived. She had been of the opinion that we all would be leaving aboard the same ship; supposedly a ship is expected to leave on June 16. But please don't count on that departure date since you may be greatly disappointed. Personally, I don't count on that date—I'd rather be surprised. I have also visited the Kollmanns. His brother wrote to him to describe how his poor mother had died when she was beyond human help. The rest of their letter was quite pleasant. In any case, the brother's family would like to join them; they believe they may be able to secure a visa for entering Italy, with the potential for earning a living there. So the Kollmanns intend to wait patiently until some possible destination opens for them.

You have written very little about your children, and with the beautiful weather you probably will have even less chance to share their presence. My only wish is to know that all of you remain healthy. Amen! So this is the end for today.

Feel kissed often and lovingly by . your Mother

23 June 1946

All my most beloved ones,

Another week has passed and, to my regret, I cannot report anything new. Just for a change I went to the Consulate where the consular official told me, "You'll just have to wait until you get a letter from the Consulate!" As a result I decided to go to the UNRRA Office to see if they could help. There their *macher*[120] told me that they could not do anything for me at this time; they had received official orders from the Consulate to try to expedite only when that particular individual was scheduled for the ship leaving on 4 July, otherwise they could not process all the people expected to leave with that ship departure date. So therefore I convinced myself with a heavy heart to wait until my turn arrives; obviously all my hysterical actions had proved useless. Yesterday a lady physician – one of my acquaintances – promised me to intervene at the Consulate on my behalf because she had a friend there. But I have very little hope that her efforts will help me. As stated earlier, all of us need some more patience! To be honest, sometimes my frayed nerves get the better of me, as does my useless life! If I at least knew how long this wait is supposed to last, I would look for some kind of job instead of idling away in the face of the good Lord. So that's enough about me, but I just had to get that off my chest!

Dear Emil, I'd like to confirm the receipt of your letter dated 6 June; I really enjoyed its news, especially the fact that your firm is anticipating the arrival of more orders. As a matter of principle, has your firm already delivered some orders? If yes, I hope that those deliveries worked out smoothly. Of course, all of this really interests me!

I am taking everything happening here to heart, but I won't complain anymore about the local inflation spiral. Yesterday I visited the Hubers again where he made the remark, "Dear lady, we have made a big mistake. We should have asked your son-in-law to do

---

120   functionary

our shopping! Then both of us would have made some money!" But I turned that offer away on your behalf, dear Emil, because you just don't have any time for this assignment; but you, dear Gusti, would have performed admirably! As your father used to say, "If you understand something too late, then you don't have anything!" Many people have huge amounts of money that they would love to invest. There is an unbelievable large inflow of many goods such as plastic purses, nylon stockings, coats, dishes, shoe soles, etc. All of this is available in immense quantities here; some of this merchandise is even sold by street vendors! Initially, all this merchandise was extremely expensive; but by now these prices have been lowered considerably due to the oversupply of these goods. For example, at first nylon stockings were up to $40; now you can buy them for $16. So people say that you could have made a mint if you had been here early enough! But now it's much too late, even if you move to Australia and don't start at such a huge scale. But that's enough for this topic! I just wanted to briefly describe some of the local business conditions.

So now it's your turn, dear Rudi! I cannot confirm the receipt of any of your letters, and I am not annoyed at you if none is on its way! I am convinced that both you and dear Käthe are more than busy, and that Käthe needs to think of more important matters related to opening your own business. Hopefully you could open your office on time so that you were able to handle your first patients. I hope wholeheartedly that everything fell into place and that you have achieved some success. I needn't tell you that all my thoughts are with you! Hopefully you don't take it too hard if initially things are not working out as you had hoped for. Obviously you know that the tastiest food takes time to bake! Of course I am also very interested in how you have arranged things in your household and for the children. You cannot imagine how it hurts me to while my time away over here when I could really help you out. I am compelled to always return to this key thought, but to everyone's regret nothing can be changed right now. Day before yesterday, I received a letter from the Hellers who could not praise you enough, dear Käthe! Of course, I am overjoyed to hear such news! But there just aren't enough words to discuss your helpful role on their behalf. If other people in a much better position would be equally helpful then the world would be a much better place, particularly for the Jews! I also received a very nice letter from Lore after a long pause; I plan to respond to her immediately. I also received a letter from Mrs. Liebling that took almost four months to arrive. She would like to send her very special regards to you, dear Gusti.

Now Lieserl is about to have a birthday; I am quite certain that it will be duly celebrated. *Nebbich* I had hoped to be there to attend. So I want to congratulate you too. I hope that you can continue to enjoy your children! Tell me everything that happened! Of course I was with you in spirit! So then the next birthday will be Henry's; that birthday will be particularly important! And so time just passes. I can still remember the children the way they used to be, but they have grown a lot in the meantime.

I was quite interested in the newspapers that you, dear Gusti, sent; then I gladly delivered them to the people for whom you had intended them. But I just didn't want to bother you with their requests. I get a chance to read the Aufbau at Mrs. Eitelberg. So in that way I can save you some effort and money. Obviously, we really study the Aufbau from front to back! With respect to American fashions, we are not surprised by them because the people here also seem to stick to the American styles. And over here people seem to go "naked" during the very hot summer season: No stockings, no hat, and very little else. Right now we can get along well because it's quite cool at night, but it will get even hotter later on. But we will have to bear these hot spells. *Mazel Tov* to you, dear Gusti, on passing your driving test. So now you just have to practice a lot! When I read about your daily program, I just get dizzy! Have your guests left already? Then the peace and quiet will seem completely unusual. So now your children will get their report cards; I just hope that you will be satisfied with all their grades and not cause a fuss. Are you, Rudi, going away on a vacation?

Apparently that time off doesn't seem as urgent as in New York. Or perhaps you get away on your own? What's going on with Karl and Elli? Hopefully they are luckier than I. Up to now no parcel has arrived; but just within the last few days a ship arrived with mail and the Aufbau. If the parcel doesn't arrive now, it may have been sent back. And then there is nothing anybody can do. But please don't send me anything! Perhaps I will be able to leave; if the parcel doesn't come, I can buy anything and everything over here—perhaps more easily than you can! I am very sorry to hear that Gerhard was not discharged from the Army. Hopefully he won't have to return to the Far East. I am saying that only from his point of view because the local summer certainly is no picnic! The military forces have been reduced substantially over here; but perhaps things will change and I will no longer enjoy his company.

Mr. Stein wrote me a letter to announce his presence. He has asked me to bring him two kimonos for his daughter. But I had to tell him no in accordance with your request; I will be traveling with only two small suitcases, without really knowing how many of my possessions I'll be able to bring with me. I just hope that he is not offended but I just cannot really help him. I'll take care of straightening out this matter. I presented our picture of the Kagran factory to Mrs. Dr. Stein since I cannot see how I can bring it with me. Father really treasured that picture! That was the only thing left with us from the factory. Actually the picture had been ruined when stored in a suitcase when a can of tomato sauce exploded. The tomatoes left a big spot on the picture that Father tried very hard to remove, but was unsuccessful. I am certain that Mrs. Stein will call you, my dears. She is well informed about everything happening to you since I visit them every week. But she remembers only very little. She seems to be generally well, but she no longer is a child at age 78. The Demuths who are quite familiar with my tale of woe are also supposed to call you. Mrs. Deutschberger told of her instinctive feeling that I will be traveling with them, but I am convinced that this won't happen, as much as I would want to do so. Marianne Stern visited me on Saturday a week ago. She made me a present of some very beautiful winter gloves; she is a very sweet person. She is always interested in all my doings. She is a very diligent person while running the production for Mrs. Kann's knitwear products; in addition, she served as Mrs. Herz's interim boss of the workshop for about four weeks when Mrs. Herz was away because of her husband's death. She is very capable and can serve in any position when necessary. He also earns a little bit of money so that they can sort of muddle through. Every Friday I visit the Engels. So I have my schedule that my weeks can pass by.

My case at the Consulate does not involve the Consul; he is a charming young man. The normal immigration quota is not applicable for me; so therefore they cannot tell me anything here. Obviously, the situation in Europe seems to take up most of the available quota; therefore life isn't easy for the local staff. So I am still in the habit of saying that the Jews are *nebbich* always in dire need! Just think of the absolutely glorious time while my parents were alive! And even though there were some wars during their life times, can anybody compare them to today? By now I have *schmoozed* enough! With all my heart I want to wish you good health and success in your business ventures! By the way, I don't remember if I congratulated you, dear Rudi, on your raise! In any case, I was very happy to hear about that event. Did you get that raise at your boss's initiative, or did you have to "push him"? So now that's the end!

Feel kissed often and lovingly by your loving   Mother

Western Union Cablegram to Glaubers. July 18, 1946

VISA RECEIVED TODAY DEPARTURE ABOUT END OF AUGUST

AM VERY HAPPY LOVE MOTHER

IDENTIFICATION CARD	
S.S. MARINE LYNX	
CABIN CLASS	
Name	MRS. E. MAYER
Shanghai to	PACIFIC COAST
Cabin No.	HOSP. AREA *B48-33*

The final stamp in Erna's passport is: REPUBLIC OF CHINA August 7, 1946.

She arrived in San Francisco on August 25, 1946

Erna, Helen and Hank in Oakland 1946

APPENDIX

KÄTHE'S STORY — IN HER OWN WORDS
(In English)

February 6, 1978

When my granddaughter, Suzanne, asked me if I would talk to her high school history class about my experiences under Hitler, I said, "yes, gladly." When she recently reminded me of my promise, I decided I better take inventory of my memories.

In my memory the years during which Hitler came to power in Germany in 1931, to the carefully planned takeover of Austria in March 1938, were largely a time of anxiety and fear of what the future would hold for my family and me.

During that time we traveled in Switzerland and France, where we met many people who had left Germany because their lives and means of support were threatened. Their stories sounded unbelievable. Why should anyone, who never harmed anybody or did anything wrong at all, be persecuted, physically attacked, jailed and tortured?

Everybody knew that the Austrians were not like the Germans. We could not be forced to march in goose steps, following "The Leader." "It cannot happen here" was the general reaction to what was happening just a few hundred miles away. However, growing unrest among the working population brought the rude awaking that an excellently organized underground movement had succeeded. They promised those who had little to lose that their participation in a take-over would make them instantaneously owners of businesses, leaders and managers and give them power that they had never had.

This unrest forced the Austrian government to call a plebiscite for Sunday, March 13, 1938. Thursday, before the 5 p.m. radio newscast, there was suddenly an interruption, with the news that the Nazi armies had crossed the borders, taken over all government buildings, taken prisoner all political leaders and called off the plebiscite. The shocking news ended abruptly with the words, "May God help Austria," and a record of the Austrian hymn, then silence. From that moment on everybody knew that lives were in jeopardy, that all the tales of atrocities might come true here. Now, whoever had friends or relatives in foreign countries, preferably overseas, feverishly started writing for affidavits, boat or train fares, promising never to be a burden to the sponsors. Immediately borders were closed and nobody could leave the country without a certificate that Reichsfluchtsteuer (a tax on property leaving the country), had been paid.

For myself and my family the time from March until September, when we left for America, was a chain of chaotic shocking experiences. Five days after take-over we were rudely awakened by the loud sound of the night bell at the building where we lived above my husband's office. The night watchman opened the gate to a group of uniformed Nazis and two policemen who had an order to take my husband into protective custody. We knew that resistance only would have provoked the Nazis to brutality, so my husband chose to go with the policemen quietly. The children slept through our tearful goodbyes. An hour later the group was back to do a house and body search which included not only the rooms, beds, drawers but also physical body search of myself, and my aged mother-in-law. These searches became routine and after three nights of it we preferred to lay awake waiting for the bell, followed by harassment, and questioning, regarding hidden money. Meanwhile uniformed Nazis were posted around our building while their leaders tried unsuccessfully to run the business, The First Vienna Laundry and Linen Supply, established by my husband's grandparents.

After a week it was decided to release my husband long enough for him to teach the new leaders how to run the business. Two months later the gestapo picked him up from the office and he was taken to former army barracks called Rossauer Kaserne. I did not know his fate until the next morning. There he joined two other men in a cell that was 9 feet by 9 feet wide. The food consisted of bread and soup three times daily. There was no interrogation, no way for contact with the outside world, just lying on the floor, lights on all night, plus hourly roll call. The families were not allowed to visit, but could write post cards, which was some consolation.

The three men, as well as other inmates kept in similar cells did their best to keep their morale up by talking about their families, possibilities to emigrate, making playing cards from toilet paper and chessmen from bread.

Meanwhile, I was advised that if my husband would give his business to the Nazi regime he could get a certificate that would enable him to leave the country, however, without any money at all. We were fortunate that a cousin, who we had met on our honeymoon in Rome, had kept contact with us. She understood the gravity of the situation and wired us that an affidavit was on the way to the American Consulate. When I went there, hundreds were standing in line only to be told to "go home, don't call us, we will call you." That was little help. Unless we could leave the country we certainly would be deported to the notorious concentration camps. Fortunately at that time we only knew part of the truth, and did not realize that the road to the camps were mostly "one way streets."

By coincidence, a few days later I received another affidavit from a cousin in Stanford who mailed it to me directly instead of following the correct procedure to send it to the Consulate. This affidavit gave me tremendous moral support. I took it with me to the gestapo headquarters, located in an elegant downtown hotel, the Hotel Metropole. With more courage than good sense, I insisted on seeing the top man, to request release of my husband so we could leave the country. All that time I had no contact with my husband, or with anybody willing to sign the family business away. For me there was no doubt that it was the only way to save our lives. I was called back several times. The authenticity of my papers had to be checked and rechecked. I had to swear that that we would leave the country within 30 days after release of my husband, and finally he was freed. The joy of being together and alive for a while completely overshadowed the new worry, how to arrange for our transportation and how to provide for those left behind?

When the final papers for the takeover (not sale!) of the business were signed, we learned that we would be allowed money to pay for the passage—ship, train and plane fares—and the transport of our furniture.[121] We were in heaven. The fact that we were allowed only $3.00 per person to take in cash, that jewelry and other disposable valuables were to be left behind, did not bother us. We were young, we felt like pioneers, the first ones of our family to leave the country, with the best intentions to do everything in our power to bring every member of our family and all friends out who were not as lucky as we were. We were among the first arrivals from Austria in Chicago where we immediately went to work providing affidavits for as many as possible.

---

121   They shipped all of their household furnishings, including china, silverware, the grand piano, and a few small pieces of jewelry.

GUSTI'S STORY – IN HER OWN WORDS
(In English)

Responding to requests from her grandchildren and great grandchildren Gusti wrote the story of her life. She wrote about her ancestors, her childhood and her life in America.

—-Beginning on page 9 of her autobiography

"…As nice as all this sounds there were signs of changes; England went off the gold standard and that caused quite some disturbances and the 1929 stock exchange crash in the U.S. had its repercussions. Hitler's name appeared here and there and though we managed not too badly we were all thunderstruck when on March 11, 1938 Hitler's troops marched jubilantly into Austria, received as if they were liberating Austria from bondage! Though there were always signs on the walls, e.g. an over life-size picture of Hitler at the HAPAG (Hamburg-American Line office) in the Kaertnerstrasse, opposite of the Opera, fully visible through a huge glass door. My immediate reaction to this sight was: TIME TO GET OUT!!! And I said so to Emil and my parents, who all thought I was crazy. After all, Austria was such a Catholic Country, it just could not happen here. Cardinal Innitzer would see to it that "our Austria" will remain free from Hitler's plans.

Well, all of us were wrong and the lucky ones left as soon as possible and went wherever they were able to turn. People were fetched from their apartments, picked up on streets and all thrown into prisons without rhyme or reason. Members of Free Masons and B'nai B'rith were particularly persecuted. Some came out after a few days without any further explanations, some were sent to concentration camps.

Jewish families were not permitted to keep "Aryan" help; our Nini was not with us anymore but came visiting and took pride in telling us that she always cared for the graves of Hitler's parents, coming from Braunau, she knew them.

Gradually our friends left Vienna; my parents however, were convinced their devoted, decent and honest gentile neighbors will always stick up for them, nothing will happen to them. They sent Emil on trips to buy new machinery, wanted to enlarge the plant. That was too much for me. Emil was a Czechoslovakian citizen and so were we by marriage and could leave on the spur of the moment to England, France, or Belgium. England and France, allied with Czechoslovakia could be involved in a war. Should such a tragedy happen, Belgium, Holland, and Denmark, were neutral and kind, most of all Denmark and Belgium, Holland at times. Inasmuch as friends of ours went to Belgium we followed them and stayed more than a year there and love Antwerp to this day!

They were beautiful people the Belgians; they experienced the German cruelties during World War I and the Lord Mayor of Antwerp was fighting with the Socialists in Spain. They were most hospitable and kind to all and everybody who crossed their borders and helped as good as they could.

Our departure from Vienna was somewhat dramatic: surrounded by all sorts of rumors that people are fetched from homes, made to scrub streets with toothbrushes, getting whipped. I quickly decided to call my parents and Emil—it was about 10 a.m.— and advise them that I want to leave that very evening with the children,[122] leave everything behind and if Emil wants to come along he has to come home immediately. Needless to say my rather categorical demand made them speechless and after a moment of hesitation my father said, "well, child, if you think this is best, Emil will be home shortly." And he was!

Next to leave was my Grandma;[123] she recovered fairly well after a slight stroke, regained her speech and was used to say what went

---

122   George and Eleanor, were five and eight years old at that time.
123   Amalia Adler Mayer

through her mind. At that particular time that was not possible and the safest solution was to send her with a nurse to her daughter in Switzerland. She stayed with the Blochs until even Switzerland became restless and their son, teaching in Stanford, California asked them to come to California. At that point Grandma was put in a nursing home and another friend of the family, Clara Berlowitz, took care of her for a few months. She passed away shortly afterwards.

My own parents and their brothers and sisters in Vienna went their own ways: one aunt passed away, another went to her daughter in Prague to end up in a concentration camp. The younger generation went mostly to England where some of their offspring still are. They are in touch with each other and when coming to the United States we always have the pleasure to see or at least talk to them.

Eventually my parents were no longer permitted to go to the plant and one worker, employed by my father as so called caretaker of the grounds as well as working in the plant, with a small apartment in the house turned out to be the one and only registered Nazi and did his utmost to make their lives miserable.

After missing all good chances my parents went to Shanghai where my father passed away. My mother [Erna] lived mainly with my sister in California, came visiting for one or two months, but found more satisfaction to run my sister's household. She had many friends and acquaintances and was loved and revered by all who knew her. She still was able to pack a lift for us before leaving for Shanghai and thus we have some of our things with us here.

The start in the United States was difficult; however, none of us would like to miss the crazy beginnings, we all appreciate more and better what we accomplished...

EGON STERN'S LETTER
(In English)

Egon Stern was an attorney in Prague before World War II. He was the brother-in-law of Rudy Weiner's cousin, Joseph Pick. He was an accomplished pianist and organist, spoke half a dozen languages and during his later life he did translations into Czech from eighteen languages. Long before the war, Egon's parents had invested in some property in Prague with Rudy Weiner (the "*tachles*" referred to in his letter).

Dr. Egon Stern   Prague, April 13th, 1946
22 Sokolska
Praha II
Dear Rudi, dear Katerina,

After 90 months the first sign of life from you! And a happy one as I can read from your kind letter. Well, from overseas there can come only merry news, naturally. More than a marvel is a happy letter from this side of the globe and if there is one, it is only conditioned. To determine what we have suffered here would mean a thick book, quite a biblioteque. How it was possible to overlive this hell and why I have survived, it is very hard to say. My wife has often said: "So many noble Jews I have known, and you, *Haderlump*,[124] you will not give me a chance to become an interesting widow." You can be sure that all the days were filled with such jokes; neither the day in October 1941 when my poor mother was brought to the Fair Hall to be deported, nor the day when we read that the younger brother of my wife was

---

124   A lowly human being

shot for high treason, leaving a young widow, a girl of 3 years and an as yet unborn son here.

With the exception of the relatives who were "AV"/*Arisch versippt* [125] and one cousin of mine who was in Terezin[126] more than 3 years, all my relatives are dead. It is the same thing in all Jewish families in Europe. Only one percent of one percent of European Jewish stayed in their prewar habitations; my family belongs to this small rest. And from the religious point of view: nearly all European synagogues are destroyed. In Prague and in the other Czech towns of Bohemia-Moravia are all intact, but there are no Jews now. In the Districts of Mlada Boleslav from where your mother is originated or of Tabor from where I come out there are now less Jewish souls than there were Jewish communities – not families or clans 50 years ago.

With the very first day of the German invasion in March 1939 my profession has gone. 18 months later our houses were confiscated. Because of the immense rise in prices it was a wonder that we could reach with our money without making debts or selling all clothes, furniture or jewels. Some good people helped us as they could and there are many good souls among the Czechs. It was a further wonder that my wife was not forced to work in a factory; for me and the child, which was submitted to the Jewish *restrictive* laws, it would have been a catastrophe.[127] The last three months my son, a young man despite being age ten and a half and I spent in the Ghetto of Teresina; by this way we were spared the air raids of February and March 1945 which caused much damage in the town. In our house all glass broken; the suburban houses in Branik are intact.

And now some material questions, so called "*tachles*."[128] When the properties of Ida[129] and myself were confiscated, the Gestapo asked whether Mrs. Katerina Weinerova, then Katharina Weiner, is a Jew. With a courage which now seems to me a half suicide, I declared that

---

125   Married to a Christian spouse
126   Theresienstadt concentration camp
127   His wife was not Jewish at birth so she and her son were technically not Jewish even though she had converted to Judaism in 1936.
128   Tough issues
129   Egon's sister

she is a niece of the former Sudeten-German Minister Mayer. There-fore, the property of Mrs. Katerina Weinerova was not seized, but nevertheless the property's income was mixed with the other money of the Auswanderungsfond.[130] The only loss is the net income of the past 50 months and now I am fighting against the National Admin-istration to get this money back. In this case your property would be clear of debts; if not, you will have to clear it during the next 4 years, I hope. The lease was stopped on the pre-war level, but the expenses are rising up, nothing unusual in post-war Europe. But as we are far from any inflation, this discrepancy will find an end soon.

The position of the renewed Republic is innumerately better than of any other state in Europe. The expulsion of more than 3 million German-speaking Czechs gives unbelievable possibilities to the rest of the population. Prague is now the centre of the continent. A ka-leidoscope of the different uniforms, a mixture of all languages with one exception, German, strictly forbidden.

And now let us congratulate you on the largest of all marvels, the life and health of your mother.[131] Amidst the broadest family she is the only representative of the elder generation. You can never thank God enough that she was saved in the last moment from all the atroc-ities of the Teutonic terror.

As I shall have some free time again I will write you.

Meantime our loveliest regards,   Egon Stern

According to George Pick, Egon Stern's nephew:
"In 1947 (after the letter above was written) my father visited Prague on a business trip, and offered to get Egon to the United States. He turned it down. His law practice was doing very well, and he figured he could continue.

A few months later, Yehudi Menuhin came to Prague to play the violin, and his accompanist was unavailable for rehearsal. My uncle was asked to accompany in Menuhin's rehearsal. Egon had wanted to

---

130   Jewish Emigration Fund.
131   May refer to Erna Mayer or to Berta Weiner, Rudy's mother.

be a professional pianist when in university and his father insisted he get a law degree first, which he did. Menuhin apparently offered to bring him to the U.S. and offered to guarantee his immigration. He felt that Egon could earn a living playing the piano in the United States. Egon declined because he felt that Prague would be the center of the new Europe and his law practice was thriving. Eight months later, after the communist coup in 1948, he was imprisoned by the communists for defending someone who was not in favor with the state. When he was released after six months, without charges, he felt practice of the law under the communists was too risky. He then had the choice of working in the government as a lawyer, for 1800 crowns a month, or as a night watchman for 1200 crowns. He chose the latter to be less exposed. He guarded a coal warehouse at night and did translations from many languages until he retired."

ERNA'S RECIPES

The ingredients were originally measured in grams on a kitchen scale. They have been converted to cups and teaspoons. During the final third of her life in Oakland and New York, Erna created many Viennese delicacies, including Sacher Torte, Napoleons and Apple Strudel.

This is Erna's version of Linzer Torte. There are many other recipes but this one has remained the family favorite.

LINZER

2 cups finely ground walnuts
2 sticks sweet butter, softened
1 cup sugar
¼ to ½ cup ground cocoa
2 cups flour
Raspberry jam

Knead all ingredients together until well blended. Press 2/3 of mixture into a large cookie sheet. Form a small rim around the edges.
Spread with raspberry jam.
Roll out the remaining 1/3 of dough and cut or roll into narrow strips. Place diagonally in both directions (criss-cross) over the jam.
Bake about 15 minutes at 350° degrees.
Slice in squares and let cool in pan overnight.

Bischofsbrot and Gugelhupf recipes were found in Erna's cook-books. Eleanor Feitler translated and converted them into teaspoon and cup measurements.

BISCHOFSBROT

4 eggs, large
¾ cup sugar
1 ½ cups flour
¾ cup walnuts, chopped
¼ cup raisins
½ teaspoon baking powder
Grease and flour a rectangular loaf pan.
Blend nuts and raisins with a portion of the flour to prevent falling to the bottom of the cake.
Beat eggs and sugar until very foamy and light colored
Stir in remaining ingredients.
Bake in a preheated 350° F. oven for 40-45 minutes or until a cake tester, inserted in the center comes out clean and dry.
Remove from oven. Place on a cooling rack

GUGELHUPF

Butter, melted to grease pan
1/4 cup+1 teaspoon butter, unsalted
1/4 cup sugar
5 1/4 cups all-purpose flour, unbleached
.7 oz. 1 teaspoon instant yeast
2 egg yolks
4 eggs
8 ozs. milk
warm water
1/2 cup raisins (dark or light)
1/4 cup black coffee (strength to taste)
3/4 cup semi-sweet chocolate bits, melted

Using melted butter, grease and flour a gugelhopf or bundt pan thoroughly. Shake excess flour from pan.
In a small saucepan heat milk to boiling, cool. Stir in 1 Tablespoon sugar and when cooled to body temperature, the yeast.
Dredge raisins in 2-4 Tablespoons of flour.
In a large mixing bowl beat 1/2 cup butter until light and fluffy. Gradually add remaining sugar.
Beat in eggs one at a time. ADD egg yolks one at a time. (The batter may look grainy and separated)
Pour bubbling yeast into butter/egg batter. Stir by hand to avoid splashing.
With mixer on low speed, add flour and raisins. May have to stir remaining flour in by hand and several tablespoons of warm water, one at a time, beating well after each addition.
Divide dough into two bowls.
Stir melted chocolate into hot coffee until well blended
Into one bowl of batter, stir in chocolate/coffee blend thoroughly. Taste. Additional sugar may be added, if necessary.
Add one tablespoon of sugar at a time. Taste.

Using a large serving spoon, alternate dark and light dough into prepared Gugelhopf/bundt pan.

Using a knife, cut through the dough to blend the batters.

using plastic wrap and a folded dish towel, cover the pan. Set into a warm place, away from drafts to rise until doubled in bulk. This may take an hour or more.

Preheat the oven to 350 F. Bake for about 1 hour. Check the center of the pan after 45 minutes, using a skewer for doneness. If dough clings to skewer, place a brown paper bag over the top to prevent excess browning.

Gugelhopf is done when a skewer, inserted into the center comes out clean.

Cool on a wire rack upside down for 5 minutes before removing the mold/pan.

SEMMEL AUFLAUF

2 rolls
2 ½ oz butter
1 ½ oz sugar
1 ½ oz ground walnuts
1 T raisins
2 eggs
Rind & juice of one lemon
Milk

Use rolls at least two days old.
Grate the rind and set aside.
Soak rolls in milk and squeeze out all moisture.
Cream butter and sugar. Add egg yolks gradually, then rolls, raisins and ground walnuts.
Fold in stiffly beaten egg whites, lemon rind and juice and one T. bread crumbs.
Bake until golden brown at 350° in a buttered soufflé pan or pie dish.
From Austrian Cooking and Baking By Gretel Beer

NUSSBEUGEL

4 cups flour
1 tsp. salt
1 cake compressed yeast
or 1 pkg. dry granular yeast
1 ¼ cups butter
3 egg yolks
1 cup sour cream
1 tsp. vanilla

Sift flour and salt; blend in yeast and butter.
Mix yolks, sour cream and vanilla.
Add flour and mix.
Divide dough into 8 parts. Roll each part into a ball, wrap in waxed paper and chill thoroughly.
Sprinkle board and roller with confectioner's sugar. Roll each ball in a 10 to 12 inch circle; cut in 12 wedges.
Spread each wedge with 1 tsp. of the following filling:

Filling: 3 egg whites
1 cup sugar
1 ½ cups grated walnuts
1 tsp. vanilla

Beat egg whites stiff; add sugar gradually. Fold in the nuts and vanilla. Roll each wedge from wide end to the point. Bake in hot oven, 400° F for 12 to 15 minutes.
Settlement Cook Book, copyright 1954

VANILLE KIPFERLN

1 ¼ cups flour
½ c. unsalted butter
1 cup ground almonds or walnuts
1/3 cup sugar
1 tsp. vanilla

Knead all ingredients together until dough can be shaped in rolls 1 inch thick. Chill in refrigerator. Cut roll in ½ inch pieces and roll and shape into crescents. Bake on ungreased cookie sheet at 300° until light gold, about 20 minutes. Cool on sheet.
Remove and turn in powdered sugar flavored with stick vanilla.

GLOSSARY OF PEOPLE, PLACES AND INSTITUTIONS

Adler, Vilma and Hans. Cousins of Emil and Gusti; settled in Washington D.C.

Agnes Bloch. See Bloch, Agnes

Beer, Paula. A sister of Erna. Died in the concentration camp

Berta Weiner. See Mawei; see also Weiner, Bertha

Betts, Helen Weiner, Lieserl, Liesel, daughter of Käthe and Rudy, living in Kensington California in 2008

Bleier, Hans. Brother of Nelly Bleier Immergut. See Immergut

Bloch, Agnes. Sister of Hans Mayer, wife of Gustav and mother of Felix Bloch. The Blochs were living in Switzerland in the 1930's; settled in San Francisco

Bloch, Felix, Fibsi. Käthe's cousin, a son of Agnes; a sponsor of the Weiner family. He emigrated from Switzerland in 1933 and became a professor of physics at Stanford; his four children were born in Palo Alto. Felix received the Nobel Prize in Physics in 1952

Bloch, Gustav. Brother-in-law of Hans Mayer, husband of Agnes

Bloch, Lore. Wife of Felix Bloch

Bloch, Oscar (Oskar). Trude Rosenstein's brother, a cousin of Käthe, settled in Argentina

Bloch, Otto. Trude Rosenstein's brother, a cousin of Käthe. Settled in Palestine

Bubbling Well Road. Hans and Erna's address in the French Concession before they were required to move to Hongkew

Burschi. See Weiner, Otto

Clara Schoenmann. See Schoenmann, Clara

E.W.D. Erste Wiener Dampfwäscherei. A commercial laundry established by Alois Weiner in Vienna in 1872; in March 1938, when

185

the Nazi government seized both the firm and the surrounding property, it was owned by the heirs, Helen Hahn, Egon Weiss, Hans Weiss, Rudolph Weiner, Hermine (Minka) Slaton and Steffi Markus

Edi Rauchberg. See Rauchberg, Edi

Egon Weiss. See Weiss, Egon

Ellie Malz Mayer. See Mayer, Ellie Malz

Emil Glauber. See Glauber, Emil

Emma Weiss. See Weiss, Emma

Engel. Dr. Paul, husband of Seppl

Engel, Seppl. A childhood friend of Käthe Weiner, settled in Quito, Ecuador

Engelhuber. Erna's abbreviation for the families Engel and Huber who helped her in Shanghai. They had been business associates of Hans Mayer before 1938. Not related to Paul Engel.

Ernst. See Rosensteins

Feitler. Eleanor Glauber Feitler, Daughter of Gusti and Emil Glauber, married to Joseph Feitler, living in Manlius, New York in 2008

Fredi. See Mayer, Franz

Fred. See Markus, Fred.

Fritz Neubauer. See Neubauers

Georg Knoepflmacher. See Knoepflmacher, Georg

Gertie Karplus. See Karplus, Gertrude

Glauber, Emil. Husband of Erna's daughter Gusti; after his marriage to Gusti he worked as an engineer and manager of the Mayer Fabric Finishing establishment. He died in New York in 2001 at the age of 105

Glauber, Fred, Fredl. Brother of Emil; Fred was a doctor; married Susi Juer. They bought the house next door to Emil and Gusti in Forest Hills, New York. The brothers and their wives, each with two children, lived side by side for the rest of their lives

Glauber, Gusti. Erna's daughter. She died in New York in 2007 at the age of 101

Glauber, Karl. Brother of Emil, settled in New York

Glauber, Richard. Brother of Emil, settled in Israel

Glauber, Susi., Susie. Wife of Fred Glauber

Glauber, Walter. Brother of Emil, died in Auschwitz

Gustav Bloch. See Bloch, Gustav

Gusti. See Glauber, Gusti

Hahn, Hella, Helen. A cousin of Rudy, settled in New York

Hans and Edith Weiss. See Weiss, Hans and Edith

Hella. See Hahn, Hella

Helen. See Betts, Lieserl

HICEM. An acronym for three agencies aiding Jewish emigration: HIAS Hebrew Immigration Aid Society; ICA Jewish Colonization Association; and Emigdirect

Hilda, Hildusch. Wife of Rudy's cousin Georg Knoepflmacher

Hirsch, Rosette. A distant cousin of Rudy; she was a sponsor for the Weiner family, met their ship in New York, helped settle the family in Chicago, Illinois

Hitzing. The Mayer family's summer place in Vienna's thirteenth district

Hongkew. The Jewish ghetto in Shanghai. The one square mile area across the river from the International Settlement where many of the refugees had found living places before the Japanese forced them to move in among the resident Chinese

Immergut, Edi. Son of Nellie and Walter

Immergut, Nellie and Walter. Friends of Erna in Shanghai; Nellie died in a rickshaw accident in Shanghai; Walter and Edi visited the Weiners and Erna in Oakland

Joint Distribution Committee. Referred to as the Joint or JDC provided relief to Jewish refugees in Shanghai and other war torn countries

Juer, Susi. Wife of Fred Glauber

Kagran. A rural suburb of Vienna in the 22nd District

Karplus, Gerhard. Husband of Gertie. Gertie's stepsister, Ellie Malz, was married to Franz Mayer, a brother of Hans; Gerhard was a successful architect in Vienna before 1938. He emigrated to the United States, served in the United States Army and was stationed in Shanghai. He became a successful architect in New York after the war and designed an addition to the Austrian Consulate in New York in 1992

Karplus, Gertrude, Gertie. See Karplus, Gerhard

Käthe, Katinka. See Weiner, Käthe

Knoeflmacher, Georg. A first cousin of Rudy; settled in Bolivia where he became a professor of engineering

Knoepflmacher, Uli, Ulrich. Son of Georg Knoepflmacher; came to UC Berkeley in 1951 and lived for a time with the Weiners in Oakland; became a professor of English at UC Berkeley and later at Princeton in New Jersey

Kollmann, Doctor Egon and Liesl. Also referred to as Kolls, They were friends in Vienna and Shanghai and settled in San Francisco after the war

Kolls. See Kollmann

Lieserl, Liese. See Betts, Helen Weiner

Lore Bloch. See Bloch, Lore

Lore, Eleanor Glauber Feitler. See Feitler, Eleanor

Maju. Susi Juer Glauber's parents; Susi's mother died at home early in the war; her father perished later in a concentration camp

Maglau. Sophie and David. Emil Glauber's parents, died in Auschwitz concentration camp

Markus, Fred. Nephew of Rudy Weiner; he served in the U.S. Navy after emigrating from Vienna and finishing high school in the United States

Markus, Steffi Weiner Markus. Rudy's sister, who, with her husband Herman and children, Eva and Fred, came first to Chicago and later moved to Oakland, California

Mawei. Bertha Weiner. Rudy's mother, emigrated to Chicago via Cuba around 1941-42. Died in Oakland in 1961

Mayer, Ellie Malz. Wife of Franz Mayer, stepsister of Gertie Karplus

Mayer, Franz, Fredi, Fritzi. Hans's brother and partner in the fabric finishing plant in Vienna; husband of Ellie

Neubauer, Fred. Grew up in Tachau (Bohemia) alongside the Glauber brothers; settled in New York. He and Richard were lifelong friends of the Glauber brothers

Neubauer, Richard. Brother of Fred. See Neubauer, Fred

Oskar (Oscar) Slaton. See Slaton, Oskar

Paul Schratter. See Schratter, Paul

Paula Beer. See Beer, Paula

Pointroad, 1106 . Hans and Erna's address in Hongkew

Rauchberg, Edi. Close friend of Käthe and Rudy. Edi settled in Australia as Edi Rogers

Rauchberg, Willi. With brother Edi, a close friend of Käthe and Rudy; settled in San Francisco, California as Willy Rawley

Richard Glauber. See Glauber, Richard

Rosenstein, Ernst and Trude. Cousins of Käthe, were able to emigrate from Austria under the Czechoslovakian quota in 1940 and settled in San Francisco, California

Rosette Hirsch. See Hirsch, Rosette

Rudy Weiner. See Weiner, Rudy

Schoenmann, Clara. Erna's sister, died in concentration camp in 1941

Schratter, Paul. Son of Erna's Sister Auguste who died when Paul was very young; he spent much of his childhood with the Mayer family in Kagran; served in the United States Army and lives in Boston in 2008

Schurli. George Glauber, son of Gusti and Emil; living in Ohio in 2008

Slaton, Oskar (Oscar). Married to Rudy's sister Hermine, Minka; manager of the E.W.D. came first to Winetka, Illinois, later moved to Minneapolis, Minnesota to be near daughter Ruth

Slaton, Ruth. Daughter of Oscar and Minka; married Merle Harris in Minnesota

Steffi Weiner Markus. See Markus, Steffi

Susi. See Glauber. Susi

Toi toi toi. Good luck or "knock on wood."

Trude. See Rosenstein, Ernst and Trude

Uli. Ulrich. See Knoepflmacher

UNRRA. United Nations Relief and Rehabilitation Administration

Vilma. See Adler

Walter Glauber. See Glauber, Walter

Weiner, Käthe. Erna's daughter, married to Rudy. Died in Oakland, California in 2007

Weiner, Otto, later Henry, Hank. Son of Käthe and Rudy Weiner; living in Oakland, California in 2008

Weiner, Rudy. Husband of Käthe Mayer, Erna's daughter; emigrated with their two children in 1938 to Chicago, Illinois and in 1945 moved to Oakland, California where Erna joined them in 1946. He died in Oakland in 1973.

Weiss, Egon. A cousin of Rudy

Weiss, Emma. Hans Mayer's sister, not related to Rudy Weiner's cousins also named Weiss

Weiss, Hans and Edith. Cousins of Rudy, settled in New York where Hans became a successful architect.

GLOSSARY II

Erna mentioned many people whom we were unable to identify. Rather than invent their stories I have chosen to leave them to the readers' knowledge or imagination.

The Engels in Shanghai were not related to the Engel relatives who settled in Quito, Ecuador. The Shanghai Engels and Herr Ingeneur Schwarz may have been business associates of Hans before the war. They had been in Shanghai for many years before the influx of refugees between 1939 and 1941. They were not required to move into Hongkew in 1943 and were able to be very helpful to the Mayers.

Altmann
Berger
Hans Bettelheim
Bielitz
Binder-Delikat
Boeckbinder, Mrs.
Braun
Braun-Feuermann
Buchstab
Deutschberger
Deutschland (Deutsch), Olga
Duldner, Karl, Luscha, Fritz,
Hella, Kurt
Eckstein, Pauli
Eichberg
Eisler
Eitelberg, Dr.

Ellis
Engel, Ernst, Eva
Engler
Fallek
Fischer, Otto
Freud, Dr.
Fried, Liesel
Fuchs
Fuert
Gewitsch
Geiringer, Rolly
Glueckmann
Gruener, Martha
Gutwillig, Herbert, Edith
Halpern, Willi
Heller
Hirschhaeuter, Paul
Hohenberg
Huber
Joseph
Kardos
Kaufmann, Ernst
Kisch
Klebanoff
Klinger, Hans
Klinger-Taussig, Rose
Kreise
Kriegl; Mrs. Kriegl {nee Vlcek}
Laub {dental technician}
Lichtmann
Nanseck
Niepoort – Oporto
Oppenheimer
Perl, Dr.
Platschek

Por
Posamentier
Przibram, Professor
Quartiermeister
Reiner, Paula
Rittermann
Sachs, Dr.
Schnitzer.
Schwarz Brown-Boveri, Mr.
Schwarz, Herr Ing.;
Schwarzbart
Schwomer
Sedlarik
Sinai, Mrs.
Spanierman, Dr.
Strehlen
Teltscher. Miss; Kitty
von Stoery, Herr
Weiner, Margit
Weismann, Dr.
Weissberger
Weizenberg, Dr.
Wodicka.
Wottitz
Wong

BIBLIOGRAPHY

Documentation Archive of the Austrian Resistance Movement. http:// www.doew.at

Friedrichs, Dr. Theodor. *Berlin Shanghai New York.* Cold Tree Press. Nashville. Tennessee 2007

Kaplan, Vivian Jeanette. *Ten Green Bottles.* St. Martin's Press. 2002

Los Angeles Times, July 15, 1997. *Shanghai's Jews Tell Story at Last.* By Henry Chu

Ross James R. *Escape To Shanghai A Jewish Community in China.* The Free Press A Division of MacMillan , Inc. 1994

http://www.rickshaw.org/July 17htm

http://www.wikipedia.org/. Hongkew

Made in the USA
Charleston, SC
27 April 2010